W9-BLE-229

Import/Export
How to Get Started in International Trade

Dr. Carl A. Nelson

LIBERTY HALL
PRESS™

This publication is designed to provide accurate and authoritative information in regard to the subject matter covered. It is sold with the understanding that the publisher is not engaged in rendering legal, accounting or other professional service. If legal advice or other expert assistance is required, the services of a competent professional person should be sought.
—*from a declaration of principles jointly adopted by a committee of the American Bar Association and a committee of publishers*

LIBERTY HALL PRESS books are published by LIBERTY HALL PRESS, an imprint of McGraw-Hill, Inc. Its trademark, consisting of the words "LIBERTY HALL PRESS" and the portrayal of Benjamin Franklin, is registered in the United States Patent and Trademark Office.

FIRST EDITION
10   FGRFGR   9 9 8 7 6 5 4

© 1990 by LIBERTY HALL PRESS, an imprint of McGraw-Hill, Inc.

Printed in the United States of America. All rights reserved.
The publisher takes no responsibility for the use of any of the materials or methods described in this book, nor for the products thereof.

Library of Congress Cataloging-in-Publication Data

Nelson, Carl A.
Import/export : how to get started in international trade / by
Carl A. Nelson.
p.   cm.
ISBN 0-8306-4052-5 (p)
1. Commerce—Handbooks, manuals, etc.   2. Exports—Handbooks,
manuals. etc.   3. Imports—Handbooks, manuals, etc.   4. New business
enterprises.   I. Title.
HF1008.N459   1989
658.8'48—dc20   89-13021
                                              CIP

For information about other McGraw-Hill materials,
call 1-800-2-MCGRAW in the U.S. In other countries
call your nearest McGraw-Hill office.

Vice President and Editorial Director: David J. Conti
Book Editor: Nina E. Barr
Book Design: Jaclyn J. Boone
Director of Production: Katherine G. Brown

Contents

Success Stories *v*

Acknowledgments *vii*

Introduction *ix*

1 Winning the Trade Game *1*
International Trade 1
Global Changes 3
Why Get into Trade? 4
Where Do Importers and Exporters Trade? 5

2 Launching a Profitable Transaction *6*
Terminology 7
Homework 7
Choosing the Product 8
Making Contacts 10
Market Research 12
Initial Quotations 15
Pricing for the Bottom Line 20

3 Planning and Negotiating To Win *27*
The Market Plan 27
Negotiations 33
Intellectual Property Rights 35
Communications 37
Travel 46

4 Completing a Successful Transaction *50*
Financing 50
Avoiding Risk 54
Documentation 73

5 Exporting from the United States *93*
Introduction 93
Government Support 94
Export Information Sources 95
Export Controls 104
Tax Incentives of Exporting 110

6   How to Import into the United States *114*
Introduction 114
Government Support 114
Import Information Sources 115
Customhouse Brokers 117
Getting through the Customs Maze 118
How to Use the Harmonized Tariff Schedule 124
Import Quotas 134
Special Import Regulations 134

7   Setting Up Your Own Import/Export
Business   *137*
The Mechanics of Start-up 138
The Business Plan 142

8   Twenty Ways to Win Import/Export
Success   *152*

Appendices

A   Foreign Business Organizations   157

B   Foreign Commercial Services
Overseas Posts   158

C   District Offices of the United States
International Trade Administration   159

D   Customs Service Organization   160

E   United States Customs Districts   161

F   United States Government Bookstores   162

Glossary   *163*

Index   *187*

About the Author   *193*

Success Stories

Story Title	Page
Mother of Two Imports a Line of Dresses From Mexico	*11*
Swedish Exchange Student Exports Golf Clubs to Sweden	*12*
Husband and Wife Export Training Software to New Zealand	*15*
Japanese-American Exports Stuffed Toys to Japan	*32*
Woman in Mid-60s Exports Peanut Butter to Australia	*38*
Man Imports Rattan Furniture from the Philippines	*55*
Computer Whiz Exports Software by Direct Mail to South America	*100*
Construction Engineering Firm Exports Their Services	*112*
Woman Imports Bead Fringe from Egypt	*152*

Dedication

To those who dare: the American entrepreneur

"Fortune befriends the bold."
—Virgil

Acknowledgments

I accept full responsibility for any faults this book might have and gratefully share any praise for its virtues with the following persons:

Geena Clonan, owner, textile importing business; Mary Jean Del Campo, instructor, import/export school; Leonor Ferrer, owner, customhouse brokerage; Bill Green, international student; Creighton Lawhead, President, San Diego World Trade Association; Bernice Layton, Vice President, International, Greater San Diego Chamber of Commerce; Marilyn Miller, international business student; Francisco Philibert, international businessman; Richard A. Powell, Director, San Diego office, Department of Commerce; David Porter, owner, customhouse/freight forwarder brokerage; Francisco Pinell, Librarian; Rene A. Romero, owner, customhouse brokerage; Bert Salonen, Vice President International, San Diego Trust; Thomas Shelton, Assistant District Director, United States Customs Service, San Diego; Bill Stonehouse, International Director, San Diego Port Authority; and David Weiss, owner, import/export business.

These wonderful folks took time to read the draft manuscript and provide valuable constructive criticism.

Thank you.

Special Note: Addresses and telephone numbers offered in this book are subject to change.

Introduction

IMPORT / EXPORT: HOW TO GET STARTED IN INTERNATIONAL Trade is a practical book that explains the basics of international trade from A to Z, in terms anyone can understand. It deals with every aspect of importing and exporting, citing helpful details and examples. Its overall message is that doing business across national borders is not difficult and can be profitable.

WHO IS THE BOOK WRITTEN FOR?

Small-Business Owners

This book is for the managers and staffs of small- and medium-sized manufacturing and service firms who lack practical, hands-on experience and wish to learn the transaction mechanics of importing and exporting. After all, according to the United States Department of Commerce, less than 10% of America's manufacturing and service companies are involved in international trade, yet many more would participate if more employees and leaders understood the process better.

Entrepreneurs

Many people are intrigued by the thought and challenge of starting their own profitable business to market their own products, as well as others, across international borders. They see untapped markets and profits and want to know how to get into the growing business of international trade. An import/export business offers great opportunity for writing off your travel expenses and enjoying the prestige of working with clients all over the world.

Individuals or companies can act as an *international intermediary* or *middleman* (a unisex term); that is, they can sell foreign-made products in the United States (import); they can sell American products in other countries (export); or they can do both.

For exports, every manufacturer or service company, in the United States, not already selling overseas can be a potential client for you.

Conversely, for imports, you can buy goods abroad at low prices, and sell those foreign products to American consumers who are very eager to buy.

Whether you run your business from your home, do it part-time or full-time, or as an expansion of an existing domestic retail or manufacturing firm, an import/export business often requires little capital investment for startup. Combining travel and international trade is an exciting way to reap the rewards of excitement, and to touch the exotic and excellent profit potential.

Students

I also have written this book for students and others wishing to enter and pursue a career in one or more phases of international business. Teachers and professors will find it suitable as a classroom text that gives perspective and helps learners gain an appreciation of the total process and how their specific job fits into the big import/export picture.

Foreign Business People

Although the slant of this book is toward the American reader, it can be equally valuable for people from foreign countries who wish to know how to do business across the borders of the greatest market in the world.

Women

"Oh, sure, but this importing/exporting stuff is only for the Male White Anglo-Saxon Protestant (M-WASP)." No statement could be farther from the truth, because in the battle of the sexes, America is way ahead.

Around the world, it's still very much the same old *Vive la différence*. In Europe, a few women have risen through the ranks, and the farther east you go, the tougher the going gets. It's true that American women often experience a culture shock in the Middle East. Even today, they are forbidden to drive cars or ride bicycles in Saudi Arabia. In Japan, even though a few women have broken into middle management, the general acceptance and regard for women in business remains many years behind the United States.

From mailrooms to boardrooms, American women have become as commonplace as pinstripes and button-down collars. In the United States, there's more opportunity and freedom for women in business than almost any other country in the world.

More than 3 million women own businesses—22 percent of all smaller firms—which gross more than $40 billion annually.

Recently, greater numbers of women have begun to start-up or run their own businesses, and as the number has increased in the United States, the number involved in import/export has increased proportionately.

American women in international business just figure out ways to overcome the obstacles. They simply end-run the problem or go to more receptive markets. For example, women doing business in most Middle Eastern countries often arrange for men to handle their direct negotiations with Arab businessmen. One such woman flies to Alexandria, takes a room in a fine hotel, and from there directs the negotiations of her Egyptian associate. She meets the principals involved only when the deal essentially is complete.

In spite of the difficulties, there are many success stories, and women in the international marketplace are encouraging other women to join them.

New Americans

So-called minority groups, other than women—i.e., American Indians, Asians, Blacks, Hispanics, Middle Easterners, and others—often have a natural expertise which helps them *source* (find) or *market* (sell) products overseas. For them, many of the expected obstacles turn into advantages. For instance, to sell in most of Africa, it is an advantage to be a black American. Most newcomers to the United States have the advantage of speaking and understanding another language and culture. Getting off the ground in an import/export business often is easier for new Americans because contacts are already in place.

WHAT'S IN THE BOOK?

The premise of this book is that the reader knows little or nothing about importing or exporting. Therefore, this book will lead you through a transaction in a very logical process—a way no other book uses to deal with the subject.

Authors of other books separate importing from exporting, implying the two are distinctly different. In fact, the mechanics of an import or export transaction are exactly the same. Importing is just the mirror image, or *commonality,* of exporting.

I have organized this book into three parts. The first part consists of chapters 2, 3, and 4, which explain the commonalities of the transaction process. This part is applicable to people of any country, because the theory is the same anywhere in the world. In chapter 2 you will learn how to decide whether your selected product will be profitable and salable.

After you have found your niche in the phenomenal international trade business, chapter 3 explains how you should plan and negotiate the transaction. The final chapter of this section of the book reveals the methods of completing the deal, including how to avoid risk.

The second part of the book consists of chapters 5 and 6, which discuss the peculiarities of importing and exporting across America's borders. They include how to obtain approved government export licenses, as well as how to use the United States' new Harmonized Tariff schedule.

The final part of the book consists of two chapters which deal with setting up your import/export business, whether it be as an intermediary or as a department of a manufacturing or service company. It provides a suggested format for a business plan and, in the final chapter, offers 20 ways to ensure success in international trade.

The appendix of this book lists a fountain of information in valuable tables, telling you where to go for United States Department of Commerce assistance and where you can get the low-cost information that is available from your nearest government book store. The book also includes a complete glossary of the most commonly used import/export terms.

You should use this book as your primer. It will lead you through the method I've developed to make learning the basics of importing and exporting simple and possible for everyone.

COMPARING AND CONTRASTING

Unlike any previous book on international trade, this one presents my original method of learning the basics of importing and exporting in terms of comparing and contrasting commonalities and differences.

The Commonalities of a Transaction

This book cites sixteen transaction-related concepts that are common to import and export. For example, terminology and communication for exporting and for importing is identical. I have presented seven concepts in chapter 2, five in chapter 3, and four in chapter 4.

I have presented each fundamental concept in this order to facilitate your understanding of them and because it is the order in which real world transactions generally happen. Please don't, however, mistakenly assume that the order represents a hierarchy of importance, that each concept truly can stand alone, or that they always happen in this order. Each fundamental integrates with the other concepts in the process of international trade and each is equally necessary. Successful importers or exporters grasp their importance and put them to work.

The Differences

Most countries have unique laws and practices of importing and exporting. For example, in the United States, export licensing controls apply only to exporting, whereas tariff schedules relate only to importing. These distinguishing processes of importing and exporting in the United States are offered in chapters 5 and 6, respectively. This treatment should clarify any differences and enable you to understand them easily.

HOW TO USE THIS BOOK

Whether you enter international trade through imports or exports, you should understand the basics of both. The best way to use this book is to master the concepts and hands-on specifics presented in chapters 2 through 6 first.

It is unlikely that you will be ready to begin trading until you organize a business to do so. In chapter 7 you will learn how to put the fundamentals to work profitably in a business setting. At this point, the fun really begins.

The final chapter of this book (chapter 8) offers 20 secrets to import/export success—obey these and you will make big profits.

Having once read and studied this book, because of its depth and completeness, it will become your reference guide which will be there when new events occur during the operation of your business.

1

Winning the Trade Game

TRADE MEANS THAT ONE PARTY PRODUCES AND EXCHANGES GOODS and services for currency or the goods and services offered by someone else. When this exchange takes place across national boundaries, it is called *international trade.*

INTERNATIONAL TRADE

Exports are the goods and services *sold* by individuals or nations. *Imports* are the goods and services *purchased.* By these methods, products valued at more than 2 trillion United States dollars are exchanged worldwide each year. By the mid–80's the United States alone exchanged more than $600 billion in two-way trade, and sales volumes are increasing every year. When we, as consumers, enjoy fresh flowers from Latin America, tropical fruits in the middle of winter, or a foreign car, we are participants in, and beneficiaries of, international trade.

We are living in the age of global interdependence—a time of increasing expectations brought about by the worldwide distribution of Hollywood movies, New York and London television, and speedy transportation systems. People all over the world want the same luxuries and standards of every other place. They see things and, naturally, they want them.

Richard Whalen of the Center for Strategic and International Studies, Georgetown University, sees international trade as a game. In his best school-house language he suggests, "The international (trade) struggle is actually a little-understood contest among governing elites, testing relative ingenuity in devising new political and economic arrangements to offset mounting social and cultural obstacles to productivity."

As a business person, you know, when left alone, the "free enterprise" and "free market" system works. Fortunately, things are happening! More and more nations are moving toward free trade and open-market systems. International trade has become the business of the '80s, '90s, and the future.

United States of America

The United States recently passed a new trade law, called the Omnibus Trade Act, which, in many ways, stiffened the American resolve to ward off protectionist trends. That act strengthened the president's authority to negotiate for more open markets. It also, among other things, provided for less burdensome export controls and approved America's joining the rest of the international community in using a more common tariff schedule. Bilateral negotiations are ongoing to spur an increase in international business.

Canada

Effective January 1, 1989, Canada and the United States formed the world's largest free-trade area. The two countries were each other's largest supplier and customer with almost $170 billion in two-way trade in 1987. The new agreement will strengthen the existing deep and friendly relationship by eliminating all tariffs between the two countries by 1998, expanding government procurement opportunities, liberalizing laws and regulations related to services, and continuing a favorable investment climate—all of which leads to many more new trade and investment opportunities.

Mexico

Mexico has joined the General Agreement on Tariff and Trade (GATT), and that means a movement toward more open markets and a greater opportunity to sell United States products in that country—resulting in more international trade opportunities.

European Community

The twelve-member European Community (EC) is in the process of completing the formation of a Single Internal Market. By 1992, some 300 rule changes will result in the removal of substantially all physical, technical, and fiscal barriers in the exchange of goods and services from within the Common Market.

The target changes are:

- to agree on a common value added tax rate,
- to remove handicaps to market entry to allow freedom to establish financial firms and services across borders,
- to deregulate transportation,
- to establish minimum industrial and safety standards
- to broaden the EC-wide bidding process for government procurement.

This initiative could radically change America's competitive conditions in one of our largest markets, but on the overall, it should be another major change in the world of international commerce that will increase the total volume of trade.

Asia

Importing and exporting with the Pacific Rim countries has now surpassed our trade with Europe.

Nonmarket Countries

Even the nonmarket (communist) economies are moving toward free markets. China and the Soviet Union are doing more and more market business with western nations. Many eastern European countries already have established trade relationships.

GLOBAL CHANGES

The General Agreement on Tariff and Trade, a supra-international body, has entered into a complex period called the *Uraguay Round*, with the goal to change trade rules and reduce trade barriers by multilateral and bilateral negotiations. The result will be new markets worldwide. The total volume of international trade will grow even more.

Things are happening! As a result of all the changes, many American businesses are making big profits in international trade. Millions of others are asking, "Is the time right for me to get into the import /export game?"

To answer this question, let's look at the history of United States international trade. Our ex-colonial forefathers were in a trade deficit during most of the nation's early years. In fact, it wasn't until the 1880's that the balances became positive. Fifty years later, during the Great Depression, the balances shifted back to large deficits. Following WWII, America had unprecedented surpluses. We now have deficits. In 1987, the United States' merchandise trade was out of balance by $170 billion. In 1988 the deficit improved to about $140 billion. Notwithstanding the improvement, Americans were still spending $140 billion more for imported goods than America was exporting.

Even though United States imports still exceeded exports, traders gained tremendous profits, because the opportunities for profit from two-way trade depend on whether you see the glass as half full or half empty.

Optimist

The optimistic importer says, "$140 billion more imports than exports? I'm making a whole lot of money. I better stay in imports." An optimistic exporter would say, "What goes down must come up—the rate of decline is reversing. I'm staying in exports to make big profits!"

Pessimist

A pessimistic importer might say, "The deficits are reducing. It's time to begin exporting." A pessimistic exporter would say, "Overall, things look really bad for exporting. Maybe I should start importing."

Those who are winning the trade game know that regardless of deficits or surpluses, the time is always right for business in international trade to make profits. The winners simply swing with political and economic changes over which they have little or no control.

WHY GET INTO TRADE

Three reasons exist for people to get into the trade game:

1. Imports: Everyone is buying foreign—it's in vogue. Imports are bringing big profits.

2. Exports: Some experts acknowledge that exports have

been out of balance but they say that the tide has turned. These people believe that now is the time to make profits in exports.

3. Global Community: Americans are awakening to realize that the world is interdependent. People of each nation rely on people of other nations to exchange goods, services, and ideas.

How Do You Take Advantage of These Opportunies?

If Whalen is right, and international trade is a game with constantly changing rules, there will be surpluses in the future, just as before. Seen as a game, you, the participant in international trade, must do business within today's rules. In order to win the game, you must first understand the basics as presented in this book. Only then, with equal ingenuity as the governing elites, can you employ the rules to varius business applications and find methods to jump tariff and nontariff walls in order to enjoy profitable international business.

WHERE DO IMPORTERS AND EXPORTERS TRADE?

Though America has significant deficits with several of our top trading partners, we have surpluses with many other countries. The opportunity to conduct import/export is everywhere, because the world market has become much more interdependent and trade conditions among nations change rapidly. Today, conditions might favor importing with a given country, but tomorrow they could favor exporting. Realistically, international trade involves both importing and exporting, not one at the exclusion of the other.

Novices to international trade, whether companies or individuals, can get started through importing or exporting. Once trade begins, opportunities spring out of nowhere. A person who successfully starts importing very soon learns of exporting opportunities and vice versa. In any case, a person can make a whole lot of money. Two trillion dollars wouldn't be traded worldwide if it weren't profitable to do so.

The next chapter will launch you into the first steps of an import/export transaction and speed you on your way to international trade success and profits.

2
Launching a
Profitable Transaction

THE NEXT FIVE CHAPTERS EXPLAIN THE BASICS OF IMPORTING AND exporting. They apply to manufactured products as well as the growing service industries such as computer software, construction engineering, or insurance.

These basics are the bridge from producer to buyer. This bridge has been in place for many years, and so has been tested by time. Nevertheless, it is possible to perceive the fundamentals as obstacles. Don't let the learning process deter you. Anyone can learn the nuts and bolts of international trade.

This chapter addresses the first 7 commonalities of an importing or exporting transaction. If you understand these concepts, your import/export business will get off to an excellent start toward early profitability.

1. Terminology
2. Homework
3. The product
4. Contact making
5. Market research
6. Initial quotations
7. Pricing for the bottom line

Don't mistakenly assume that the order presented in this book represents a hierarchy of importance, or that these fundamentals are in the precise order of an import/export project. In reality, many things happen simultaneously; seldom does a concept stand alone.

TERMINOLOGY

Because of increasing international interdependency, trade literacy has become as important as computer literacy in modern business. As you progress in your reading, frequently refer to the extensive glossary of terms found at the end of this book. Many of these terms also are defined wherever they first appear in the text. Don't be frightened off by the new terminology—you can learn it!!

HOMEWORK

Research is one of the keys to winning the trade game! Even if you have some experience in international trade, it's unwise to jump into an unresearched project. In fact, it's not unusual to spend several weeks learning about the product and its profit potential before getting serious.

An import/export project requires you to answer 4 preliminary questions before deciding whether the project merits further investigation.

1. In what product or service are you interested? For the prospective importer/exporter, this decision is personal as well as technical. For the manufacturer of a product or provider of a service, this step is moot—you sell your own product or service.
2. To whom will you sell the product or service? And from whom will you obtain the product or service? Who are your contacts? Do you have more than one source for the product you intend to import or export? Choose very carefully the country where you intend to sell your product.
3. Are people and/or firms willing to buy this product or service? Although products and services that carry the label "Made in U.S.A." continue to be popular, they no longer sell themselves. But, if an American product has a mature market in the United States, it very likely has a market in other parts of the world. On the other hand, many foreign goods cost less, which increases   sales potential, but if the product is unique to a given culture or the quality is cheap, Americans might not buy it.
4. Do the rough calculations of price and quantity warrant undertaking the project? Determine whether the margin

of profit makes the project worthwhile. What changes must you make to the product to ensure a profitable export or import? Bear in mind that just as much work goes into importing or exporting an unprofitable product or service as trading a profitable one. Don't waste time with losers.

CHOOSING THE PRODUCT

The question asked most often is, "What product should I select to import or export? Should it be rugs or machinery?"

Keep it simple in the beginning. If your firm already manufactures merchandise or provides a service, that product or service is what you sell. But, for your own import/export business, your job will be to sell someone else's product or service. In other words, you will be the middleman.

The Personal Decision

Most people begin with a single product or service they know and understand, or have experience with. Others begin with a line of products, or define their products in terms of an industry with which they are familiar. Above all, product selection is a personal decision, but the decision should make common sense. For example, if you aren't an engineer, don't begin by exporting gas turbine engines. Or, if you are an electronics engineer, don't start with fashionable textiles.

A good example is the established American house painter who began making excellent profits exporting a line of automated painting equipment to Europe. He knew the equipment before he began.

Start your business with a product or service with which you have an advantage. You can gain that advantage because of prior knowledge, by doing library research about a product, by making or using contacts, or by understanding a language or culture.

The Technical Marketing Decisions

Keep in mind, the product you select might have to adapt to the cultures of other countries.

Product Standards. Most foreign countries have their own product standards such as flammability, labeling, pollution, food and drug laws, and safety standards, etc. Although many of these standards parallel those of the United States, you must be aware of the differences.

Technical Specifications and Codes. Most of the world uses 220V, 50 Hz, but we use 120V, 60 Hz. Similarly, most of the world uses the metric system of weights and measures. Determine how you can convert your product to meet these specifications and codes.

Quality and Product Life Cycle. The marketplace for first-generation products is dwindling. Even the least-developed countries (LDCs) want second- and third-generation models. On the other hand, in the life cycle of product innovation, manufacturers introduce new products first to developed countries (DCs), leaving an opportunity for you to make sales of an earlier model to LDCs. Assess the stage in the life cycle in which you find your export/import product.

Developed Countries Distinguishes the more industrialized nations—including all member countries of the Organization for Economic Cooperation and Development (OECD) as well as the Soviet Union and most of the socialist countries of Eastern Europe—from "developing" or "less-developed" countries. The developed countries are sometimes collectively designated as the "North" because most of them are in the Northern Hemisphere.

Least-Developed Countries (LDCs) The United Nations considers some 36 of the world's poorest countries to be the least developed of the less developed countries. Most of them are small in terms of area and population, and some are landlocked or small island countries. They generally are characterized by:

• Low per capita incomes, literacy levels, and medical standards

• Subsistence agriculture

• Lack of exploitable minerals and competitive industries.

Most LCDs are in Africa, but a few, such as Bangladesh, Afghanistan, Laos, and Nepal, are in Asia. Haiti is the only country in the Western Hemisphere classified by the United Nations as "least developed."

Other Uses. Different countries use some products for differing purposes. For example, motorcycles and bicycles are largely recreational vehicles in the United States, but in many countries, they are the primary means of transportation.largely recreational vehicles in the United States, but in many countries, they are the primary means of transportation.

MAKING CONTACTS

Importers and exporters need contacts to get started. The exporter must convince a U.S. manufacturer of his or her ability to sell the manufacturer's product or service internationally. The importer, on the other hand, must find an overseas manufacturer or middleman from whom to buy the product or service.

Contacts are classified in two categories:

1. *Sourcing* (finding) a manufacturer or provider of the product or service you wish import or export.
2. *Marketing* or selling that product or service.

The two ways to make contacts overlap. You can use them to expand your import/export network.

Sourcing Contacts

If you are an exporter, any product or service you select falls into an industry classification, and that industry very likely has an association. Almost every United States industry has a publication—if not a magazine, at least a newsletter. Begin looking for manufacturers of your product or service in the appropriate industry publication. Under "Export Information" in chapter 5, you will find other sources of information which might help you make contacts for products to export.

Contacts for importers are only slightly more difficult to obtain. Assuming you know which country manufactures your product, you need a contact in that industry in that country. Start with the nearest consulate office in the United States. Next, contact that foreign country's International Chamber of Commerce. For example, you easily can contact the Salvadoran-American Chamber of Commerce and the Australian-American Chamber of Commerce. You also can make contacts through the American Embassy or through a corresponding American industry association. Futhermore, you can make direct contact with the government of the country in which you are interested.

Next, establish communications with the contact to seek further information or to ask for product samples and prices. Usually you make this contact by letter, but you can make it by electrical means such as telex or cable. (See "Communications" in chapter 3).

Eventually, take a trip to the country with which you

intend to trade. It will make a big difference. (Travel also is explained in chapter 3).

Don't be baffled by foreign business organizations. See Appendix A to learn their names and how they commonly are organized.

> **SUCCESS STORY:** Geena Clonan, mother of two, grew up in Massachusetts. As an adult she lived for many years in Mexico City where she learned to speak fluent Spanish and to understand the Mexican culture. This advantage helped her start a profitable business importing a line of women's dresses from Mexico City to Los Angeles.

Marketing Contacts

In many ways, United States business and marketing methods and United States channels of distribution are the same as those channels and methods used in foreign countries. You would make marketing contacts through these channels.

For domestic marketing contacts, Americans use trade shows, direct sales, direct mail, and manufacturer's representatives, as well as swap meets, flea markets, home parties, or wholesalers. The United States government also will help find contacts.

> *Foreign Sales Representative* A representative or agent residing in a foreign country who acts as a salesman for a United States manufacturer, usually for a commission. Sometimes referred to as a "sales agent" or "commission agent."
>
> *Distributor* A firm that: (a) sells directly for a manufacturer, usually on an exclusive basis for a specified territory, and (b) maintains an inventory of the manufacturer's goods.

The international marketeer (trader) also can make contacts through trade shows, direct sales, a distributor an agent, who is the equivalent of a manufacturer's representative. Trade fairs or shows are often the single most effective means to make contacts and to learn about products, markets, competition, potential customers, and distributors. The term *trade show or fair* includes everything from catalog shows through local exhibits to major specialized international industry shows. At these shows, exhibitors offer literature and samples of the product.

Lists of worldwide trade shows and international conferences are available from most large airlines such as Lufthansa and Pan American as well as from the United States Department of Commerce and the United States Chamber of Commerce (COC). In the United States, your industry association will know when and where the appropriate trade shows take place.

SUCCESS STORY: A Swedish exchange student started a lucrative business exporting American golf clubs to his home country. He plays golf and knows that the sport is growing in Sweden. He already had contacts with distributors of sporting goods, so he negotiated an exclusive contract with a golf club manufacturer and he was quickly in business. Nice way to support your overseas education!!

Table 2-1 offers a range of ideas that should assist you, the importer or exporter, to make sourcing or market contacts.

MARKET RESEARCH

Market research is vital to the success of your international import/export business. Is your product salable? Does anyone care? You must be able to sell enough of the product or service to justify undertaking the import/export project. If you are presenting a new product, you might have to create a market. A good rule of thumb for the new import/export business is: "If the market isn't there, get out of the project and find another product."

International market research will save money and time. Unfortunately, too many newcomers plunge into import/export without determining whether they can sell the product at a profit.

Following are checklists of research items for importers and exporters.

Exporter Checklist

☑ Is there already a market for the product?

☑ What is the market price?

Table 2-1 Making Contacts

	Source	Market
Import	Consulate offices International COC Industrial organizations Foreign governments	Swap meets Direct mailer Mail order Home parties Trade shows Wholesalers Associations Representatives Retailers U.S. government
Export	*Thomas Register* *Contacts Influential* *Yellow Pages* U.S. Dept. of Commerce Trade journals Trade associations	Distributors Trade shows Retailers Foreign government U.S. Dept. of Commerce Direct mailer United Nations U.S.A.I.D. Sell Overseas America *Business America* State Trade Promotion Offices *Journal of Commerce*

☑ What is the sales volume for that product?

☑ Who has market share, and what are the shares?

☑ What is the location of the market; what's its size and population? People in major urban areas generally have more money than they do elsewhere.

☑ What is the climate, geography, and terrain of the market country?

☑ What are the economics of the country, its GNP, major industries, and sources of income?

☑ What is their currency? How stable is it? Is barter commonplace?

✓ Who are the employees of the country? How much do they earn? Where do they live?

✓ Is the government stable? Do they like Americans? Does the country have a good credit record?

✓ What are the tariffs, restrictions, and quotas?

✓ What are the other barriers to market entry, such as taxation and repatriation of income?

✓ What language do they speak? Are there dialects? Does the business community speak English?

✓ How modern is the country? Do they have electric power? How do they move their goods? How good is the hard infrastructure (roads, trains, etc.)? What about the soft infrastructure (schools, etc.)?

✓ Does the country manufacture your product? How much do they produce? How much is sold there?

✓ What kind and how much advertising generally is used? Are there local advertising firms? Are there trade fairs and exhibitions?

✓ What distribution channels are being used? What levels of inventory are carried? Are adequate storage facilities available?

✓ Who are the customers? Where do they live? What influences the customer's buying decisions? Is it price, convenience, or habit?

✓ What kinds of services are expected? Do they throw away or repair?

✓ What are the property right implications?

Importer Checklist

✓ Is there already a market for the product?

✓ What is the market price?

✓ What is the sales volume for that product?

✓ Who has market share, and what are the shares?

✓ What is the location of the market; what's its size and population? Major American urban areas are generally where the people have more money than elsewhere.

☑ Who are the wholesalers?

☑ What sort and how much advertising generally is used? Are there local advertising firms? Are there trade fairs and exhibitions?

☑ What distribution channels are being used? What levels of inventory are carried? Are there adequate storage facilities available?

☑ Who are the customers? Where do they live? What influences the customer's buying decisions? Is it price, convenience, or habit?

☑ What kinds of services are expected? Do they throw away or repair? Can repair services be set up?

☑ What about competition? Do they have sales organizations? How do they price?

☑ What are the property right implications?

The answers to these questions are available through most good libraries, the Department of Commerce's International Trade Administration (ITA), the United States Chamber of Commerce, or private market research companies. (See chapters 5 and 6 for a list of export and import information sources.)

SUCCESS STORY: An American husband and wife team who specialize in management training programs are making big profits exporting their service to New Zealand. Their research (homework) showed that that small country has a growing market (need), little domestic expertise, but sufficient money to pay for management training services.

INITIAL QUOTATIONS

Initial quotes begin with a "request for quotation" (RFP) sent by the importer to the exporter or with an unsolicited offer from the exporter. A simple letter or telex can be a request for a quotation. Figure 2-1 shows a sample letter of inquiry.

A pro forma invoice is often the document you would use to respond to a request for pricing information. The pro forma invoice, a normal invoice document visibly marked "Pro Forma", is the method you would use most often to initiate negotiations. Its purpose is to describe in advance certain items and details. Once accepted by the purchaser, it becomes a

Our Company, Inc.
Hometown, U.S.A.

Ref:
Date:

Your Company, Ltd.
2A1 Moon River
Yokohama, Japan

Our company is a medium-sized manufacturing company. We are interested in your products.

Please send us a pro forma invoice for five of your machines, C.I.F. Los Angeles. Please indicate your payment terms and estimated time of delivery after receipt of our firm order.

Sincerely,

W.T. Door

President

Fig. 2-1   A typical letter of inquiry.

binding sales agreement or legal contract, and the seller is bound to the terms stated. Carefully think through any terms entered on this document. Figure 2-2 is an example of a pro forma invoice.

Pro forma Invoice A provisional invoice forwarded by the seller of goods prior to a contemplated shipment advising the buyer of the kinds and quantities of goods to be sent, their value, and important specifications (weight, size, etc.).

XYZ Foreign, Co.
2A1 Moon River
Yokohama, Japan

Our Company, Inc.
Hometown, U.S.A.

Purchase Order Date:
Invoice Date:
Invoice Ref. No.: PRO FORMA 00012

Terms of Payment: Confirmed
Irrevocable Letter of Credit
Payable in U.S. dollars

Invoice To:
Ship To:
Forwarding Agent:

Via: Country of Origin:

QUANTITY	PART NO.	DESCRIPTION	PRICE EACH	TOTAL PRICE
10	A2Z	Machines	$100.00	$1,000.00

Inland freight, export packing & forwarding fees $ 100.00

  Free alongside (F.A.S.) Yokohama $1,100.00
  Estimated ocean freight $ 100.00
  Estimated marine insurance $ 50.00

  C.I.F. Long Beach $1,250.00
Packed in 10 crates, 100 cubic feet
Gross weight 1000 lbs.
Net   weight   900 lbs.
Payment terms: Irrevocable letter of credit confirmed by a U.S.
bank. Shipment to be made two (2) weeks after receipt of firm
order. Country of Origin: Japan.
We certify this pro forma invoice is true and correct.

Issu A. Towa
President

Fig. 2-2   A typical pro forma invoice.

Terms of Sale

In the domestic United States market, it is customary to quote, Free On Board (F.O.B.) factory. But in international business, suppliers use entirely different pricing terms, called *Terms of Sale*. Either of two versions of these terms might be specified so long as both parties agree: INCOTERMS-1980; or Revised American Foreign Trade Definitions-1941.

If, when drawing up the contract, buyer and seller specifically refer to INCOTERMS or to the Revised American Definitions, they can be sure of defining their respective responsibilities. In so doing, buyer and seller eliminate any possibility of misunderstanding and subsequent dispute. You can order a copy of INCOTERMS for about $10.00, from: The ICC Publishing Corporation, Inc., 125 East 23rd St. Suite 300, New York, NY 10010. You can order Revised American Definitions from The National Council of American Importers, the National Foreign Trade Council, or the Chamber of Commerce of the United States, 1615 H Street, N.W. Washington, D.C.

Following are the four most commonly-used terms of sale in international trade (to understand the many variations of these, read INCOTERMS).

***C.I.F.* (cost, marine insurance, freight).** is used to a named overseas port of import. The seller is responsible for charges up to the port of final destination.

***F.A.S.* (free alongside a ship).** is usually followed by a named port of export. A seller quotes this term for the price of goods that includes charges for delivery alongside a vessel at the port. The buyer is responsible thereafter.

***F.O.B.* (free on board).** is the quote that, unlike F.A.S., includes the cost of loading the product aboard the vessel at the named point—a port or inland point of origin.

Marine Insurance An insurance that will compensate the owner of goods transported on the seas in the event of loss if such loss would not legally be recovered from the carrier. This insurance also covers overseas air shipments.

Specific Delivery Point A point in sales quotations which designates specifically where and within what geographical locale the goods will be delivered at the expense and responsibility of the seller (e.g., F.A.S. named vessel at named port of export).

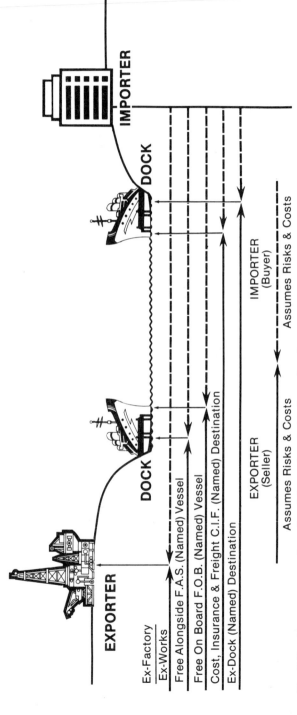

Fig. 2-3.   Here you see where the risks and costs begin and end.

EX **(named point of origin, e.g., Ex-Factory, Ex-Warehouse, Ex-Destination).** means the seller agrees to cover all charges to place the goods at a specified delivery point. From that point on, all other costs are for the buyer.

INCOTERMS are used most widely. These pricing terms clearly define the geographical point where the risks and costs of the exporter stops and those of the importer begins. Figure 2-3 graphically shows examples of these terms.

PRICING FOR THE BOTTOM LINE

Profit is an internal, individual decision which varies from product to product, industry to industry, and within the market channel. Desireable profit relates to the goals you plan for your import/export business. For instance, one person's goal might be to cover their expenses, take a small salary, and be pleased if the business supports their travels to exotic places. Another might have the goal to expand a business to eventually become a major international (vice trading) company. Yet another might set their goal to work for only 5 or 6 years, sell the business at a profit, and retire on the capital gain.

The Market Channel

In general, the international market channel includes:

• The manufacturer

• The foreign import/export agent

• Any distributors (wholesalers)

• Any retailers

• The buyers or customers

Figure 2-4 shows pictorially how this channel might look.

The price of your product should be high enough to generate a suitable profit but low enough to be competitive. Ideally, the importer or exporter should strive to buy at, or below, factory prices. You can achieve this goal by eliminating from the overseas price the manufacturer's cost of domestic sales and advertising expenses.

Each step along the market channel has a cost. If a product is entirely new to the market or has unique features, you might be able to command higher prices. On the other hand, to gain a foothold in a very competitive market, you should use marginal-cost pricing. *Marginal-cost pricing* is the technique of setting

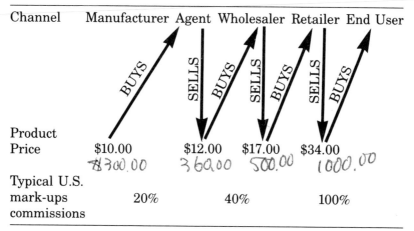

Channel	Manufacturer	Agent	Wholesaler	Retailer	End User

Fig. 2-4   A market channel.

the market entry price at, or just above, the threshold at which the firm would incur a loss. Most new importers/exporters simply use the domestic factory price plus freight, packing, insurance, etc. Prices might be quoted in United States dollars or in the currency of the buyer. In general, you should base pricing on long-run profit-maximizing objectives. Target market share and volumes for the long-term export commitment.

It is important that you understand not only the elements that make up your price but also those of your overseas trading associate. Remember, there are no "free lunches"; everything has a cost.

Figure 2-5 illustrates how a product could move from one country to another by an importer or exporter. In particular, it shows how the selling price in one country becomes the buying price in the other. Typical commission percentages are between 7% and 20% for an export middleman and between 5% and 20% for a import middleman (foreign distributor or agent), although commissions might be as low as 1% and as high as 40%. The key issues are the price of the product and the number of units (sales volume) that you can sell. If, for instance, the product is a *big ticket item* (high sales price), the commission might be quite low. A small percentage of a million dollar sale can be very good business.

Table 2-2 shows a set of fictitious costs associated with a C.I.F. quotation which corresponds to the steps shown in Figure 2-5. You can use Figures 2-6 and 2-7 as work lists to aid you in accurate costing of your product.

Is there sufficient profit at the *volumes* (number of units)

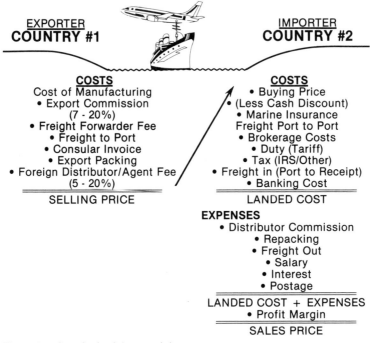

Fig. 2-5. A typical pricing model

you can sell to make it worth your while and meet your personal profit goals? Recall that the same amount of work goes into importing or exporting a product that makes no profit as one that makes a good profit. (A word of caution for manufacturers: If at first exporting doesn't appear profitable, check your manufacturing costs. It might be necessary to import less-costly components in order to compete internationally.)

Now that you are satisfied that you have a viable project, the next step is to lay out a written, long-range market plan. The next chapter explains how to develop that plan, then how to put it into action to make a transaction.

Table 2-2 Business Plan Outline

Terms of Sale: C.I.F.				
EXPORT			**IMPORT**	
Pricing Elements	**Cost**	**Pricing Elements**		**Cost**
Factory cost of 100 units @ $100/unit	$10,000	Landed cost CIF		$14,950
Expenses:		Duty @ 5.5%		$ 776
		Tax (IRS or other)		$ 150
Brokerage costs	$ 100	Brokerage		
Export packing	$ 150	clearance fees		$ 50
Freight to port	$ 500	Reforwarding		
Consular invoice	$ 50	from broker		$ 100
Freight forwarder		Banking charges		$ 50
fee	$ 150	Letter of credit		
		¼%		$ 75
*Export agent commission @ 15% of cost	$ 1,500	Total landed cost		$ 16,151
*Foreign agent commission @ 5% of cost	$ 500	Expenses		
		Warehouse		$ —
		Repacking		$ 100
		Freight out		$ 100
		Advertising		$ 500
		+Salary		$ 1,410
		Interest		$ —
		Postage		$ 100
Marine insurance (12,950 @ $1.20 per $100 value	$ 155	Total landed plus expenses		$ 18,361
Transportation (Ocean)	$ 1,000	Unit cost	= $	183
Landed cost (C.I.F.)	$14,950	Suggested selling price @ 100% markup	= $	366
		Profit	= $18,300	

*Only if an export middleman or import agent is used
+Calculated at a commission of 10% of buying price

$$\text{Markup (\%)} = \frac{\text{Sell-cost}}{\text{cost}} \times 100$$

Reference Information
Our Ref. _____   Customer Reference _____

Customer Information
Name _____   Cable Address _____
Address _____   _____
        _____   Telex No. _____

Product Information
Product _____   Dimensions____x____x____
No. of Units _____   Cubic Measure____ (sq. in.)
New Weight _____   Total Measure _____
Gross Weight _____

Product Charges
Price (or cost) per unit _____ x units _____ Total _____
Profit (or Markup)   _____
Sales Commissions   _____
FOB Factory   _____

Fees—Packing, Marking, Inland Freight
Freight Forwarder   _____
Financing costs   _____
Other charges   _____
Export Packing   _____
Labeling/Marking   _____
Inland Freight to   _____
FOB, Port City (export packed   _____

Port Charges
Unloading (Heavy Lift)   _____
Loading (aboard ship)   _____
Terminal   _____
    Consular Document (check if required) _____
    Certificate of Origin (check if required) _____
    Export License (check if required) _____
FAS Vessel (or airplane)   _____

Freight
Based on _____ weight _____ measure
Ocean _____ air _____
Rate _____ Minimum _____ Amount _____

Insurance
Coverage required _____
Basis _____ Rate _____ Amount _____
CIF, Port of destination

Fig. 2-6   A typical export costing worksheet.

Reference Information
Our Ref. _____   Customer Reference _____

Customer Information
Name _____   Cable Address _____
Address _____
_____   Telex No. _____

Product Information
Product _____   Dimensions ____x____x____
No. of Units _____   Cubic Measure _____ (sq. in.)
Net Weight _____   Total Measure _____
Gross Weight _____

    NOTE: IF QUOTE IS FOB FACTORY USE EXPORT COSTING
        SHEET TO DETERMINE PRICE AT CIF, PORT OF
        DESTINATION

Landed Cost (CIF, Port of destination)   _____
Customs duty   _____
Customs House Broker Fees   _____
Banking Charges   _____
Taxes: Federal   _____
      State   _____
      Other   _____

Total landed   _____

EXPENSES:
Inland Freight (from port city)   _____
Warehouse costs   _____
Repacking   _____
Inland Freight (from warehouse)   _____
Advertising/promotion   _____
Overhead (% of annual)   _____
Salary (% of annual)   _____
Loans (Principle/Interest)   _____

Total landed plus expenses   _____

Unit cost   _____

Selling price   _____
Margin ____%

Profit   _____

Fig. 2-7   A typical import costing worksheet.

3
Planning and Negotiating to Win

IN THIS CHAPTER YOU WILL LEARN HOW TO TAKE THE NEXT STEPS in your import/export transaction. To this point, you already have answered the following questions:

1. What product or service will you import or export?
2. To whom will you sell the product or service? And from whom will you obtain the product?
   a. Who are your contacts?
   b. In what countries and/or United States regions will you market the product?
3. Are people and/or firms willing to buy this product or service?
4. Do the rough calculations of price and quantity warrant undertaking the project?

This chapter expands on the basics of international trade in the context of the concepts that are common to moving ahead with your chosen importing or exporting transaction. The five commonalities presented in this chapter are:

1. The Market Plan
2. Negotiations
3. Intellectual Property Rights
4. Communications
5. Travel

THE MARKET PLAN

Once you have determined that your project is viable, write a long-range market plan, then execute it.

Make certain to integrate the international plan with the firm's overall strategic business plan. See chapter 7 ("Setting Up Your Own Import/Export Business") for details about how to write a business plan.

Use the following logical, step-by-step process to write your market plan:

1. *Objectives*
Examples:

- Sales of $XXX,XXX.00 by the end of the second year

- Expansion into countries 2 and 3 by the end of the third year

2. *Specific tactics*
Examples:

- Radio advertising in two cities

- Three direct mailings to each company/person on a specific list

3. *Schedule of activities or action plan*
Examples:

- A list of trade shows indicating which you will attend, including dates and duration of trips to visit overseas distributors, with their names, addresses, and phone numbers.

- Specific assignments of responsibility (An essential feature of an action plan).

4. *Budget for accomplishing the action plan*
Include every conceivable cost associated with marketing the product. Don't scrimp because this is where most start-up firms underestimate. Initial marketing costs will be high.

Segmenting the Market

Marketing segmentation enables an import/export organization to choose its customers and fashion its marketing strategy based on identified customer wants and requirements and on the response to the firm's specific desires and needs. You should perceive segmentation on a macro and a micro level.

Macro From the Greek word Makros meaning long. It is a combining form meaning large.

Micro From the Greek word mikros meaning small. A combining term meaning little, small, microscopic.

Macrosegmentation. divides a market by such broad characteristics as industry shipments, location, firm size, etc. An import macrosegment might be the dividing of a city into marketing segments. On a larger scale, it might involve dividing the United States into regions, prioritizing those regions, then developing a microplan for each region.

Export macrosegments might include prioritizing continents or countries within a continent; better yet, export macrosegments might sort by language, purchasing power, or cultural preference.

Microsegmentation. finds the homogeneous customer groups within macrosegments. Microsegmentation therefore seeks to find out who makes the decisions for each homogeneous group. Microsegmentation pinpoints where (by address) and who (by name) makes buying decisions. From this analysis, you can design a promotional strategy to target the decision-making units (DMUs).

An import microsegmentation might take the data from your market research effort and identify where the wholesalers are located. If you list and prioritize these decision makers by name and address, you will have a very logical, specific plan of attack for your marketing effort.

Your marketing plan and schedule should cover a 3- to 5-year period, depending on the kind of product(s) you market, your competitor(s), and your target market(s). Be sure to write this plan no matter how small the import/export project. Only when it is in writing will it receive proper attention and receive adequate allocation of funds.

Executing the Market Plan

Next comes the fun—putting the plan into action—actively marketing the product through trade shows, advertisements, television promotions, and direct mail—all in accordance with your budgeted plan. Remember, nothing happens until something is sold.

Personal Sales

The two basic approaches to selling internationally for imports and exports, are direct and indirect sales. Using the *direct sales method* a domestic manufacturing firm has their own marketing department that sells to a foreign distributor or retailing firm and is responsible for shipping the goods overseas. The *indirect sales* method uses an middleman, who usually assumes the responsibility for moving the goods. You may sell directly to retailers or to distributors/wholesalers. Regardless of your targeted DMU, keep in mind that international sales are just like domestic sales: someone makes a personal contact and presents a portfolio, brochures, price lists, and/or samples to potential buyers (decision makers).

Making sales requires persistence and determination. Follow-up, then follow-up again.

The Trade Show

The international trader attends trade shows for five basic reasons:

1. To make contacts
2. To identify products for import or export
3. To evaluate the competition (often done without exhibiting)
4. To find customers and distributors for import or export
5. To build sales for existing distributors

HOT TIPS ON TRADE FAIRS

- If exhibiting to sell, don't overcommit. You might get more business than you can handle reasonably.

- If searching for products to import, don't buy until you have done your homework!

- Take more business cards to the trade show than you think you will need. Have your telex number on your card.

- Obtain language help from a local university or college.

- If you are exhibiting to sell, consider prior advertisement to let potential customers know you will be there.

Trade Missions

If you are attending for the first time, consider using the fair as the keystone of the trip. Allow time afterward to visit companies you meet at the fair.Trade missions are trips made for the express purpose of promoting and participating in international trade. The Department of Commerce organizes several kinds of trade missions for exporters.

Special Missions. Are organized and led by the Department of Commerce with itineraries designed to bring you into contact with potential buyers and agents. You pay your own expenses and a share of the costs of the mission.

Seminar Missions. Are similar to the specialized trade mission; however, seminar missions add several one- or two-day technical presentations to the trip by a team of United States industry representatives.

Industry-Organized, Government-Approved Trade Missions. Though Chambers of Commerce, trade associations, or other industry groups organize these missions, the Department of Commerce adds official sanction and provides assistance prior to, and during, the trip.

Catalog Shows and Video/Catalog Exhibitions. These missions are the least expensive way to develop leads, to test markets, and to locate agents, because you don't have to be there. You simply send along product catalogs, brochures, and other sales aids to be displayed at exhibitions organized by United States embassies and consultants.

Video/catalog exhibitions are ideal for promoting large equipment and machinery which are costly to ship. The Department of Commerce organizes the exhibitions 20 to 30 times a year, and participants pay only the amount necessary to cover the department's costs.

Advertising

All countries advertise to communicate with customers. Exporters and importers must ask themselves whether advertising is important to sales and affordable. The assistance of an agency familiar with the market environment you wish to target could be critical to the success of your advertising campaign. Some countries do not carry television and radio advertising. Additionally, cultural differences often require more than a simple translation of promotional messages.

In countries where illiteracy is high, you might prefer to avoid such written forms as magazines, concentrating instead on outdoor advertising such as billboards, posters, electric signs, and street car/bus signs. These reach wide audiences in most countries.

> **SUCCESS STORY:** When the value of the dollar fell in comparison to the yen, a Japanese-American who had contacts in Osaka and experience in the toy business, saw an opportunity to export to Japan. He discussed it with his wife and his Osakan friends. They chose stuffed toys as their product, then they developed a well-defined market plan to penetrate the Japanese market. Why? Because there was a need—kids in Japan love stuffed animals—and their profit margin was excellent.

Distributors

A *distributor* is a merchant who purchases merchandise from a manufacturer at the greatest possible discount and resells it to retailers for profit. The distributor carries a supply of parts and maintains an adequate facility for servicing. The distributor buys the product in his own name, and often pays on a credit basis. A written contract usually defines the territory to be covered by the distribuutor, the terms of sale, and the method of compensation (see "Avoiding Risk" in chapter 4). The distributor usually performs the work on a commission basis, without assumption of risk, and he might operate on an exclusive or a nonexclusive basis. He usually establishes his contract for a specific time frame such that it might be renewable, based on satisfactory performance.

As with domestic sales, foreign retailers usually buy from the distributor's traveling sales force, but many buy through catalogs, brochures, or other literature.

Importers and exporters seldom sell directly to the end user. It is not recommended because: (a) it is time consuming, and (b) it leads to goods being impounded or sold at auction when the buyer doesn't know his or her own trade regulations.

Checklist

What you want from a foreign representative:

☑ A solid reputation with suppliers and banks

☑ Financial strength

☑ Experience with the product or a similar product

☑ A sales organization

☑ A sales record of growth

☑ Customers

☑ Warehouse capacity

☑ After-sales service capability

☑ Understanding of business practices

☑ Knowledge of English and the language of the country

☑ Knowledge of marketing techniques (promotion, advertisement, etc.)

Checklist

What the foreign representative wants from you:

☑ Excellent products

☑ Exclusive territories

☑ Training

☑ Parts availability

☑ Good warranties

☑ Advertising and merchandising support

☑ Credit terms, discounts, and deals

☑ Commissions on direct sales by the manufacturer in the distributor's territory

☑ Minimum control and/or visits

☑ Freedom to price

☑ Deal with one person

☑ Security that the product will not be taken away once it is established in the territory

☑ The right to terminate the agreement when he or she pleases.

NEGOTIATIONS

Americans are accustomed to a fixed-price system. We usually pay what is advertised on the label or we don't buy at all. However, many countries are on the barter system, and most people of other nations understand bargaining much better than we do. For instance, when a trader receives a quote, it is just the beginning of negotiations. For most Americans, the quote is the end. Pay for it, or don't buy it.

Bargaining

Bargaining or negctiating is integral to international trade and an importer/exporter should be ready to offer or ask for alternatives using simple letters or the telex.

In the highly-competitive international business world, a trader's ability to offer reasonable terms to customers might mean the difference between winning and losing a sale. Become thoroughly familiar with "terms of sale" as well as the other aspects of "Risk Avoidance" (explained in chapter 4).

Agreeing to a Contract

After obtaining the initial quotations as explained in chapter 2, the next step in any international business arrangement is to reach an agreement, or a sales contract, with your overseas partner. The agreement must specify terms for the cost, quality, and delivery of the product. Quality can be assured only by someone seeing the product, but cost and delivery terms are the result of a quote agreed to by the seller.

Exporters are finding it increasingly necessary to offer terms ranging from cash against shipping documents, to time drafts, open accounts, and even installment payments spread over several years. More sophisticated ideas such as countertrade, counterpurchase, and after-sales service are also negotiables.

Let your banker, freight forwarder, or customhouse broker review the final offer or quotation. A second pair of experienced eyes can save you money. (See chapters 5 and 6 respectively for an explanation of the freight forwarder and customhouse broker).

In Japan, young executives role-play negotiations before they make an initial quote. They form teams, sit around a table with a chalkboard nearby, and pretend to negotiate the deal. Each team has a set of negotiating alternatives related to the country they are pretending to represent. Sometimes they cut their offer price by 10%. If that doesn't work, they cut it another 5% or 10%. Other ploys are: (a) offer lower-interest-rate loans than their competitors. (b) offer better after-sales service warrantees, or (c) provide warehouses for parts. Sometimes, even the cost of advertising can make the difference in the sale.

Countertrade International trade in which the seller is required to accept goods or other instruments of trade, in partial or whole payment, for its products.

Counterpurchase One of the most common forms of countertrade in which the seller receives cash but contractually agrees to buy local products or services as a percentage of cash received over an agreed period of time.

Shipping documents Commercial invoices, bills of lading, insurance certificates, consular invoices, and related documents (explained in chapter 4).

Draft The same as a "bill of exchange." A written order for a certain sum of money to be transferred on a certain date from the person who owes the money, or agrees to make the payment, (the drawee) to the creditor to whom the money is owed (the drawer of the draft). See glossary, "Date draft", "Documentary draft", "Sight draft", "Time draft".

The American trader also must have a list of alternatives ready. Keep negotiations open and don't firm them up on paper until you have reached a general agreement.

The following is a partial list of alternatives and conditions you might wish to consider during negotiations:

- Quantity price breaks (Don't offer just one price)
- Discounts for cash deals or even down payments
- Offer countertrade to those countries short on foreign exchange
- Guaranteed loans
- Low-interest loans
- Time payments
- Home-factory trips for training

During your negotiations make sure you stay on the right side of the Foreign Corrupt Practices Act (FCPA) of 1977. In essence, this act makes it illegal for companies to bribe foreign officials, candidates, or political parties. Make certain that everything is in the contract and has a price; don't get caught making illegal payments or gifts to win a contract or sale. The penalties are severe—subject to a 5-year jail sentence and a fine of up to $10,000.

The law does not address itself to *facilitating payments*, those small amounts used in most countries to expedite business activities euphemistically called "mordida," "grease," "baksheesh," "cumsha," or "squeeze." Nevertheless, you should exercise great care in this regard as well.

INTELLECTUAL PROPERTY RIGHTS

"The Japanese stole my stuff! They just drove down the road, passed our factory, and copied our trademark. It took us two and a half years and $5000.00 to get it back," said one executive. Because this company had the trademark registered, no one else in the United States could use it, and the litigation against the guilty Japanese firm was considerably easier than had it not been properly registered.

Intellectual property is a general term that describes inventions or other discoveries that have been registered with government authorities for the sale or use by their owner. Such terms as patent, trademark, copyright, or unfair competition fall into the category of intellectual property.

You can obtain information about Patents and Trademarks from the United States Patent Office by calling (703) 557-HELP or writing

PATENT AND TRADEMARK OFFICE
Division of Patents and Trademarks
Washington, DC 20231

You can order the booklet entitled General Information on Patents from the Government Printing Office. Table 3-1 is a summary of the basic elements of intellectual rights in the United States.

You should recognize that registration in the United States does not protect your product in a foreign country. In general, protection in one country does not constitute protection in another country. The rule of thumb is to apply for, and register, all intellectual property rights in each country where you intend to do business. Registration can be expensive; therefore, several multilateral organizations have been formed that make it possible to make applications covering all member countries.

Table 3-1 Intellectual Property Rights

	Patents	Copyright	Trade and service marks	Trade Name	Trade dress	Trade secrets
Duration (yrs)	14–17 years	Life + 50 years	As long as in use	As long as in use	As long as in use	Until public disclosure
How	Apply to Patent Office	By original creation in perma- nent form	By use	By use	By use	By security measures
Req'ts	Useful/ novel	Non- functional original creation	Fanciful and disting- uishing	Non- confusion with others	Fanciful nonfunc- tional	Not known
Prevents	Manuf'r use or sale	Copying or adapting	Confusing or mislead'g use	Confusing or mislead'g use	Confusing or mislead'g use	Disclosure
Protects	Utility and Design Attributes	Author- ship	Reputation and goodwill	Goodwill	Reputa- tion	Info for competitive advantage
Examples	Product/ mechanism/ process/ Style	Label design/ operating manual	Coca Cola	Computer- land, Inc.	Container shape	Formula
Legal Costs	$1,500– $3,000	$10–100	$100– $400			

Patent Registration

1. The European Patent Convention (16 European-area countries).
2. The Community Patent Convention (9 EEC countries).
3. The Patent Cooperation Treaty, which gives by far the

greatest international coverage (more than 25 signature countries, including the U.S.S.R.).

SUCCESS STORY—PROPERTY RIGHTS: Dolly Doyle, in her sixties, decided that she was too young to retire. She started a business exporting her special peanut butter to Australia, a country where she often vacations, and has made many friends and business contacts. One of the first things she did was register her trade mark, "Gone Troppo," in the United States and Australia. From her investment came a lucrative business that allows Dolly to travel down under several times a year.

Trademark Registration

This procedure is less costly and time consuming than patents.

1. The International Convention for the Protection of Industrial Property, better known as the Paris Union, is 90 years old. It covers patents as well as trademarks. Under this convention, a firm receives 6 month's of protection, during which time you can register the trademark in the other member countries.
2. The Madrid Arrangement for International Registration of Trademarks has 22 members, but it offers the advantage that registration in one country qualifies as registration in all other member countries.

COMMUNICATIONS

Although nothing substitutes for personal contact when developing an international marketing structure, this might not always be possible. Therefore, the tone of initial written communications is critical. It often makes the difference between a profitable, long-term arrangement and a lost opportunity.

The Introductory Letter or Telex

Most often you can write your introductory letter or telex in English. With the exception of Latin America, English has become the language of international business, but use simple words. If you are translating or transmitting the letter or Telex into a foreign language, make sure you have it translated back to English by a third party before sending it. However proficient a person is in the other language, funny things can happen in translation.

From the beginning, establish your company's favorable reputation, and explain the relationship that you seek. Describe the product you want to market (export) or to purchase (import). Propose a personal meeting and offer the buyer a visit to your firm during the person's next visit to the United States. Ask for a response to your letter. Figure 3-1 shows a sample letter of introduction.

Follow-up Communications

As technology improves, more alternative forms of communications become available, and choosing the best alternative might result in the competitive difference. Successful importing/exporting depends on reliable two-way communication. It is critical in establishing and running an import/export marketing network.

Telephone

Speech is the fastest way to convey ideas and receive answers. Voice communications allow for immediate feedback—quick response to fast-breaking problems or opportunities. Worldwide, you can dial 95 countries directly. The rates for international telephone service range from about $1.00 to $2.00 for the first minute, (depending on the time of day) and about $1.00 a minute for each additional minute. While international telephone can be expeditious, it can be very expensive if you have a lot to say.

Telex

Telex is the most common transmitter of printed material. Currently Telex terminals are in over 2 million government and business offices worldwide. Telex units can receive information automatically, even when unattended. Handle all your communications over a Direct Distance Dial(DDD) phone line. A dedicated telex terminal costs as little as $1000.00, and they are as easy to use as a typewriter.

Telex charges are based on *transmission time*—the time you actually use the circuit. It is possible to transmit up to 1800 characters (about 180 words or more) per minute at the price of a telephone call. The carrier charge varies from $1.00 to $3.00 per minute, with service charge costs of about $3.00 per minute.

Our Company, Inc.
Home Town, U.S.A.

Ref:
Date:

Your Company, Ltd.
2A1 Moon River
Yokohama, Japan

Gentlemen:

Our Company, Inc. markets a line of highway spots. When secured to the centerline of highways these spots provide for increased safety for motorists. We believe that these spots may interest foreign markets, especially the Japanese market. Our major customers include highway contractors and highway departments of the states of ABC and DEF.

Our Company, founded in 1983, has sales of $1.5 million. Further details are given in the attached brochure. The attached catalogs and specification sheets give detailed information about our products.

We are writing to learn whether: (1) Your Company has a requirement to purchase similar products for use in Japan; and (2) Your Company would be interested in representing Our Company in Japan.

Don't hesitate to telephone if you need further details. We look forward to meeting with representatives of Your Company about our highway spots.

Sincerely,

W. T. Door
President

Fig. 3-1   A sample letter of introduction.

International record carriers (IRC's), store and forward carriers, or network services can handle a Telex.

IRCs. These companies handle international telex, cablegrams, and mailgrams. Major IRCs are Western Union, RCA, TRT, ITT, MCI, GRT, and FTCC. No significant differences exist in IRC international telex costs. IRCs are the source for telex numbers.

Store-and-forward. These carriers use batching techniques and specialize in telex transmission for companies that send five or more messages a day. Examples of store-and-forward carriers are VITEL, IBCS, and IMS. You can save more than 20% on your international telex bill by using one of these companies.

Network Services. These companies provide electronic mail services and specialize in bringing organizations and people together who have similar interests.

By custom, Telex messages are brief. Standard abbreviations and terminology are widely understood.

When you compare

TKS UR TX N TEL CALL RCNTLY. SEE U AT ARPRT TUES 3.9.88

With

THANKS FOR YOUR TELEX MESSAGE AND TELEPHONE CALL RECENTLY. I WILL SEE YOU AT THE AIRPORT ON TUESDAY, THE THIRD OF SEPTEMBER, 1988.

You can easily see the need for abbreviations.

Table 3-2 lists many of the common abbreviations. Figure 3-2 shows a sample telex message.

When you draft messages that include tables or other columnar information, consider that each space is a chargeable character up to the carriage return. The general rule is that horizontal space is expensive, but vertical space is not. It takes but 2 characters—carriage return and line feed—to skip a line. Use line skipping generously to separate logical units and to give length to the received message to make it easier to handle.

Table 3-2 Commonly Used Telex Abbreviations

ADS	address	NBR	number
ANS	answer	NL	night letter telegram
CFM	confirm	NR	no record
CHGS	charges	OFC	office
CK	check	OGNL	original
CST	cost	OK	agreed
DLD	delivered	PLS	please
DLR	deliver	R	received
DLY	delivery	R	are
DSTN	destination	RE	reference
DUP	duplicate	RGDS	regards
FM	from	RPT	repeat
GOVT	government	SGD	signed
HW	herewith	SPL	special
ICW	in connection with	SVC	service
	(concerning)		
INTL	international	TKS	thanks
LT	letter telegram	TLX	telex
MGR	manager	U	you
MK	make	WD	word
MGS	message	YR	your
N	and		

For example, compare

DESCRIPTION	QTY	PRICE
LEFT HANDED WRENCH	1	11.78
BOX	2	7.52

with

QTY	PRICE	DESCRIPTION	
1	11.78	LEFT-HANDED WRENCH	
2		7.52	BOX

TRT

188912 ATSD UT

1243 9/16

GA

20801 MYMCO TH

188912 ATSD UT

ATTN: MR. CHIEHAT PONG

PLS SEND SAMPLES N CST INFO FOR RINGS GOLD AND
SILVER
RGDS

W.T. DOOR

OUR COMPANY

U.S.A.

TEL: (AREA CODE) XXX-XXXX

FAX: (AREA CODE) XXX-XXXX

188912 ATSD UT

Fig. 3-2   A sample telex message.

Cables

You can send international mailgrams, telegrams, or cables anywhere mail goes. It requires a complete mailing address, including any postal codes. Again, IRCs handle telex, cablegrams, and mailgrams. As stated earlier, the IRCs are Western Union, RCA, TRT, ITT, MCI, GRT, and FTCC.

Cables are sent electronically, often from telex, to the major city nearest the recipient. There, the message might be telephoned and mailed, mailed only, or (in a few locations) delivered by messenger. Cables don't offer proof of delivery that a telex message does, and because of the extra handling, cables are significantly more expensive than telex messages. But you can send a cable to anyone, anywhere. Rates for cables vary by destination from $.14 to $.35 per word or character string. You can send cables via MARISAT (Maritime Satellite) to the Master, crew member, or passengers of most commercial vessels.

Facsimile

FAX, or telecopier service, has grown the fastest in the 1980s and, in many cases, it offers a large savings over telex. An advantage of FAX over telex is that you can transmit any image of up to 8 1/2 x 14 inches directly to the receiving unit. You can send letters, pictures, contracts, forms, catalog sheets, drawings, and illustrations—anything that would reproduce in a copy machine.

History Note

FAX is not new. Alexander Bain, a Scottish clockmaker, invented it over a century ago, in 1842. His devise used a pendulum that swept a metal point over a set of raised, metal letters. When the point touched a letter, it created an electrical charge that traveled down a telegraph wire to reproduce on paper the series of letters the pendulum had touched. Wire-service photos were transmitted by FAX as early as 1930. The United States Navy used them aboard ship during World War II for the transmission of weather data.

The earliest FAX machines were clunkers and were very expensive, taking more than 10 minutes to send a single page and costing more than $18,000. Today, the more than 600,000 FAX machines in the United States are expected to increase in number to more than 1,000,000 by 1990. The reason for the explosion is the improvement in cost and transmission time. Dedicated facsimile terminals now cost as little as $1,300.00 and you can lease them for about $50.00 a month. Their speed equates favorably to telex. On the down side, there are still fewer FAX machines worldwide than telex and, if your recipient has none, you can't use yours.

FAX charges include a per-page fee, a small setup charge, and any actual telephone line charges incurred. Worldwide, FAX transmits over the ordinary voice-phone network. Several private bureaus manage FAX's worldwide service. Like cable, there is no effective proof of delivery of a FAX document.

Service Bureaus

These companies, available in most large cities, provide the use of their equipment and lines so that you can send and receive telexes and facsimile. Typically, for a nominal monthly fee (as little as $10.00 a month), an import/export firm can use the service bureau's telex number on letterhead and business cards, and they can use their equipment to transmit and receive information. Telephone dictation often is available also.

Communications Equipment

Data transmission will grow rapidly throughout the 1990s. As an international marketing network develops, data must flow back and forth among the import/exporter and agencies, distributors, and customers. You must decide whether you'll be wiser to purchase your own equipment or to use a service bureau. The volume of messages will dictate the break-even point for a growing international import/export organization. If you send less than one message per day, a service company is your best bet.

When your message volume grows to more than one message per day, consider purchasing equipment and transmitting your own messages. Electronic mail is now commonly delivered over international phone lines. You can interface practically any computer (even personal computers) by a modem via a cable, ordinary telephone, satellite, or microwave to any another computer or word processor anywhere in the world so long as the receiving country does not restrict or prohibit transborder data flows. If you have a personal computer, a modem and software package can cost you less than $300.00 for data and telex communications. Keep in mind that if you use your computer as a terminal and a word processor, you will have contention for terminal time.

If competition for personal computer time begins to compete adversely with the word processer or the accountant, consider a dedicated FAX or Telex terminal. Personal ownership of dedicated facsimile or telex machines eliminates service bureau charges; however, you must consider line and equipment capitalization costs.

Hot Communication Tips

1. Write out your message and check it by reading it aloud.
2. Some situations in international business can be frustrating, so take care not to lose your temper and send

a "zinger" that you'll regret later. Develop a cordial and professional style, and stick to it at all times. Try to draft replies in the morning when you are fresh. Whenever possible let a second party read each message.

3. Send messages earlier in the day and earlier in the week to avoid the heavy calling periods and possible delay of your message.

4. Keep your messages brief, but avoid any abbreviation that might not be understood.

5. Remember that Telex is UPPER CASE ONLY and does not provide for dollar signs ($) or percent signs (%), among others. For $ use USDOL, and for % use PCT.

6. Cables are generally more expensive than telex messages. You are charged for them by the word, and words have a maximum of 10 characters. Eleven characters count as 2 words.

7. Use mailgrams rather than telegrams in the United States of America. They're less expensive and usually just as fast.

8. Try to reply to every telex message the same day you receive it, even if only to give a date when you will send a more complete reply.

9. Use "ATTN: Name" rather than "DEAR Name" and almost all telex messages, by custom, end with "REGARDS," "BEST REGARDS," or occasionally "CORDIALLY."

10. If you use an IRC (ITT, MCI, RCA, etc.) for a telex number, make sure you provide your own phone line. If the IRC bills you for line access, you usually pay double the phone company costs.

11. For direct telex connections, use the carrier that provides you with your telex number. Using another carrier will add an interconnect surcharge to your call.

12. Once you recoup your initial capital investment, shop around for services. Don't get stuck with one service. You can recoup a minimum service charge quickly by switching to a company that can lower the cost of paper mail or telex services.

13. Though print lacks speed (compared to voice), it provides written documentation that can be read and reread at the reader's pace and schedule.

TRAVEL

Mistrust across international borders can be a barrier to a successful import/export business. Therefore, visit the country and the people who offer goods for your importation or the agents or distributors who market your export products. These personal contacts remind us that we have more in common with people from other nations than differences. Traveling to exotic places is not only fun, it is a tax-deductible expense of international trade as well. The Internal Revenue Service will look closely at travel expenses to make sure you are actually doing business, and not indulging your travel hobby. For this purpose, keep a good record during your travels, and make sure you profit from your trips.

Planning a Trip

Though an agent will help you with your travel plans, don't turn over to the travel agent the initial planning of your trip. Using an Official Airlines Guide (OAG) and a map of the world, lay out your own trip. You know your itinerary, how long you can stay in each place, and what you expect to accomplish. The OAG, which can be found in any library or travel agency, will show all the direct (no change) flights, as well as all the connections for all the world's airlines. Make certain your local arrival time allows for time changes and scheduled business meetings. Allow time for rest prior to negotiating.

After you have laid out the trip, take it to the travel agent for booking. Allow three to five days and expect some changes. You might occasionally need to go through country B in order to get to country C.

Travel Danger Alert. To stay alert to any possible danger areas in the world, contact the Citizens Emergency Center at the United States Department of State, Washington, DC at (202) 647-5225.

Packing for a Trip

Travel light. The usual arrival sequence is Immigration followed by Customs. Be ready to open your luggage and sometimes declare each item.

Transportation

Request Business Class to most countries; it's more comfortable than coach and less expensive than First Class. How-

ever, one traveler remembered the time the Pakistani lady sat
next to him with five boxes, two kids, and a cage full of chickens.
In some Middle European and Eastern countries, it's better to
pay the difference and go First Class.

Hotels

Unless you are familiar with the better hotels in a country,
you are usually better off to stay at one that is recognized
internationally. Most major travel companies, agents, or your
local library can give you the names of the best hotels.

Food and Drink

Are you a bit overweight? Now is the time to drop a few
pounds. The food might be the best in the world, but eat light
and drink only sterilized water.

Time Changes

Plan for the changing time zones. Think ahead and figure
the local times of arrival for the plane you have booked. Remember, time is rezoned from Greenwich, England, and watches
normally are set to some form of zone time. Time is changed
near the time of crossing of the boundary between zones, usually at a whole hour. If you know the time zone, you can
calculate the local time. Figure 3-3 depicts international time
zones as they appear at noon, Eastern Standard Time.

Passport

This travel document identifies the holder as a citizen of
the country by which it is issued. In the United States, the
Department of State issues passports. You can apply at your
local United States post office. The cost is about $42.00. You
should allow about two to three weeks for processing the passport.

Visa

A *visa* is an official endorsement from a country a person
wishes to visit. You must receive it before entry into that
country is permitted. Some nations don't require a visa. Check
with your travel agent or local counsel/embassy. You might
prefer to give a "visa service," your passport and three photos,
and let them make the rounds of the Washington, D.C. embassies. Count on waiting a week for the completion of this service.

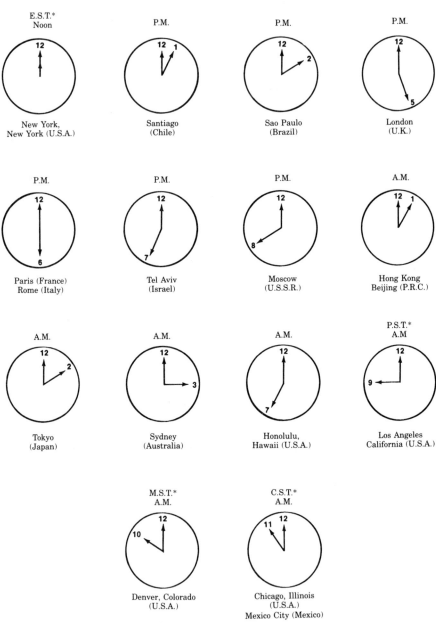

Fig. 3-3   The international time zones.

Arrival/Departure

On arrival in a country you have never visited before, ask the airline crew or counter personnel for such tips as normal taxi fare from the airport to the hotel, sights to see, and local travel problems. Exchange your currency at the best rate. On departure use the excess to pay your hotel bill. Be sure to save enough local currency for taxi fare and airport departure tax. Smile and be cheerful as you pass through immigration and customs. A smile can head off a lot of problems.

Carnet

Use an ATA Carnet to get your business samples and other equipment through customs. The initials "ATA" are a combination of both French and English words meaning "Admission Temporaire/Temporary Admission." In the United States, make application to the Council for International Business; it has offices in major cities such as San Francisco, Los Angeles, and New York.

A *Carnet* is a special customs document to simplify and streamline custom procedures for business and professional travelers. It guarantees payment in case of failure to reexport. Commercial samples, advertising material, medical or other professional equipment, whether accompanied by a person or not, may be taken under this system into participating countries for up to 1 year. The applicant must furnish security in the amount of 40% of the total value of all items listed on the application form. The fee schedule ranges from a minimum of $50.00 to as much as about $200.00 depending on the value of the merchandise. If you don't get a Carnet, check your samples at the airport with customs, but allow plenty of time to get them before the next flight.

The next chapter further expands the concepts related to import and export, developing the fundamentals needed to complete the transaction, i.e., financing, avoiding risk, shipping, and documentation.

4

Completing a Successful Transaction

NOW YOU ARE READY FOR THE STEPS NEEDED TO COMPLETE AN import or export transaction. In chapter 2 you learned the fundamentals of start-up. Chapter 3 led you through the concepts of planning and negotiating a transaction. This chapter covers the four remaining basic commonalities; that is, paying for it and physically moving the goods.

1. Financing
2. Avoiding Risk
3. Physical Distribution (Packing and Shipping)
4. Documentation

FINANCING

Why do we need financing in the import/export business?

To start, expand, or take advantage of opportunities, all businesses need new money sooner or later. By new money, we mean money that we have not yet earned, but which can become the engine for growth.

For the importer, financing offers the ability to pay for the overseas manufacture and shipment of foreign goods destined for the United States market. For the exporter, financing could mean working capital to pay for international travel and the marketing effort. New money also can be loans to foreign buyers so that buyers can purchase an exporter's goods.

American importers seldom have problems finding financing. United States dollars are plentiful, and if you do the homework phase well and you have purchase orders for the product(s), banks or factors are waiting to assist.

The Bank

Commercial banking is the primary industry that supports the financing of importing and exporting. Selection of a banking partner is an essential part of the teamwork required for international trade success.

When shopping for a bank, look for the following:

1. A strong international department
2. Speed in handling transactions (Do they want to make money on your money—called the *float*?)
3. The bank's relationship with overseas banks (That is, do they have corresponding relationships with banks in the countries in which you wish to do business?)
4. Credit policy?

Forms of Bank Financing

Loans for international trade fall into two categories: secured and unsecured.

Secured Financing. Banks are not high risk takers. To reduce their exposure to loss, they often ask for collateral. Financing against collateral is called *secured financing* and is the most common method of raising new money. Banks will advance funds against payment obligations, shipment documents, or storage documents. Most common of these is advancement of funds against payment obligations or documentary title. In this case, the trader pledges the goods for export or import as collateral for a loan to finance them. The bank maintains a secure position by accepting as collateral documents that convey title such as negotiable bills of lading, warehouse receipts, or trust receipts.

How a Banker's Acceptance Works. Another popular method of obtaining secured financing is the Banker's Acceptance (B/A). This method involves a time draft presented to a bank by an exporter. The bank stamps and signs the draft "accepted" on behalf of its client, the importer. By accepting the draft, the bank undertakes and recognizes the obligation to pay the draft at maturity, and has placed its creditworthiness between the exporter (*drawer*) and the importer (*drawee*).

Banker's acceptances are negotiable instruments that can be sold in the money market. The B/A rate is a discount rate which is generally 2 to 3 points below the prime rate. With the full creditworthiness of the bank behind the draft, eligible B/As attract the very best of market interest rates. The criteria for eligibility are:

1. You must create the B/A within 30 days of the shipment of the goods
2. The maximum tenure is 180 days after shipment
3. It must be self-liquidating
4. You cannot use it for working capital purposes
5. The credit recipient must attest to no duplication

Unsecured Financing. In truth, unsecured financing is for those companies which have a sound credit standing with their bank or have had long-term trading experience. It usually amounts to expanding existing lines of working credit. For the small importer/exporter, the bank probably will limit unsecured financing to a personal line of credit.

Factors

A *factor* is an agent who will, at a discount (usually 5% to 8% of the gross), buy receivables. In the United States, banks do 95% of the factoring; private specialists do the remainder. The factor makes a profit on the collection and provides a source of cash flow for the seller, albeit, less than if the business had held out to make the collection itself.

For example, suppose you had a receivable of $1000.00. A factor might offer you a $750.00 advance on the invoice and charge you 5% on the gross of $1000.00 per month until collection. If the factor makes the collection within the first month, he would only keep $50.00 and return $200.00. If it takes 2 months, the factor would keep $100.00 and return only $150.00, etc.

The importer benefits from having the cash to reorder products from overseas. For a manufacturer, the benefit can be cash flow available for increased or new production.

Other Private Sources

The Private Export Funding Corporation (PEFCO) was established in 1970 and is owned by 54 banks, seven industrial corporations, and an investment banking firm. PEFCO operates with its own capital stock, an extensive line of credit from the United States government's EXIMBANK, and the proceeds of its secured and unsecured debt obligations. It provides medium- and long-term loans, subject to EXIMBANK approval, to foreign buyers of United States goods and services. PEFCO generally deals in sales of capital goods with a minimum commitment of about $1 million—there is no maximum.

Government Sources

The global debt problem has had a deleterious impact on United States exporters. Many nations are short on foreign exchange, and what they have is earmarked for priority national imports and to service large international credit commitments. Nevertheless, because the United States government and various state governments are assisting in managing the debt crisis and its impact, more sources of competitive financing are available today to support exporting than at any other time in our history. The major complaint is that not enough firms are taking advantage of the programs.

Small Business Administration (SBA)

Under the SBA's regular (7A) guarantee program, small companies that can show reasonable ability to pay can get seven-year working capital loans for about 2.25% over prime. The maximum maturity might be up to 25 years, depending on the use of the loan proceeds. The SBA's export revolving-line-of-credit guarantee program provides preexport financing for the manufacture or purchase of goods for sale to foreign markets and to help a small business penetrate or develop a foreign market. The maximum maturity for this financing is 18 months. The SBA, in cooperation with the Export-Import Bank, participates in loans between $200,000 and $1,000,000 with a maximum maturity of 18 months.

Export-Import Bank

For those exporters who have found a sale, but the buyer can't find the financing in her or his own country, the Export-Import Bank has funds available to provide credit support in the form of loans, guarantees, and insurance for small businesses. Rates between 9.85% and 12.25% are available for a 5- to 10-year maturity period for both goods and services. The Medium-Term Credit Program has more than $300 million available for small businesses facing subsidized foreign competition. The Small Business Credit Program has about $7 billion available, with direct credit for exporting medium-term goods; competition is not necessary. The Exim Working Capital Program guarantees the lender's repayment on capital loans for exports.

The Agency for International Development (AID)

This organization, a subordinate division of the United States State Department, provides loans and grants to Third World nations for developmental and foreign policy reasons. Under the AID Development Assistance Program, more than $2 billion are available at rates of 2% and 3% over 40 years. The AID Economic Development Fund has about $3.5 billion, at 2% and 3% interest rates. Generally, these funds are available through invitations to bid through the *Commerce Daily Bulletin*, a publication available from the Government Printing Office, Washington, D.C. 20402.

The International Development Cooperation Agency (IDCA)

This organization sponsors a Trade and Development Program (TDP), which provides approximately $21 million on an annual basis for friendly countries to procure foreign goods and services for major development projects. Often, these funds support smaller firms in subcontract positions.

SUCCESS STORY: A Philippino man, who became an American citizen, still had many island contacts. He started his successful rattan furniture import business by obtaining an SBA guaranteed bank loan.

AVOIDING RISK

Doing business across international borders always involves risks related to financial exposure. However, avoiding or controlling risks in global trade is an everyday occurrence for importers and exporters, and understanding the instruments available for avoiding risk is not difficult. Essentially four kinds of risks exist:

BUSINESS or
COMMERCIAL   Not being paid; nondelivery of goods;
              insolvency or protracted default by the buyer;
              competition;
              and disputes over product, warranty, etc.

FOREIGN
EXCHANGE   Foreign exchange fluctuations

POLITICAL   War, coup d'etat, revolution, expropriation,
              expulsion, foreign exchange controls, or
              cancellation of import or export licenses

SHIPPING   Risk of damage and/or loss at sea or via
              other transportation

Most risks allow for a method of avoidance. Of course, there is no insurance for such problems as disputes over quality or loss of markets due to competition, but there are avoidance instruments for three aspects of risk: not being paid, insurance, and foreign exchange exposure management. Though uncertainty is natural in doing business across international borders, you can hedge and control most of it. All major exporting countries have arrangements to protect exporters and the banks who provide their funding support.

Avoidance of Business Risk

The seller wants to be certain that the buyer will pay on time once he has shipped the goods, and he wants to minimize risk of nonpayment. But the buyer wants to be certain the seller will deliver on time and that the goods are exactly what the buyer ordered.

These concerns most often are heard from anyone beginning an import/export business. Mistrust across international borders is natural; after all, there is a certain amount of mistrust even in our own culture and domestic market. One key to risk avoidance is a well-written sales contract. In chapter 2, you learned that an early step in the process of international trade is to gain agreement between yourself and your overseas business associate. This agreement should include method of payment.

Getting Paid

Ensuring prompt payment often worries exporters more than any other factor. The truth is that the likelihood of a bad debt from an international customer is less than from an American company. It might surprise some people that the foreign bad-debt ratio is less than half of the United States ratio. In the United States, the average bad-debt ratio often runs 1.25% or more of sales. In the experience of most international business-men, overseas bad debts seldom exceed .5% of sales. The reason is that, in the United States, credit is a way of life. In overseas markets, credit is still something to be earned as a result of having a record of prompt payment. Use common sense in extending credit to overseas customers, but don't use tougher rules than for your American clients.

The methods of payment, in order of the risk to the seller, are: open account, consignment, time draft, sight draft, author-ity to purchase, letter of credit, and cash in advance.

Open Account. The *open account* is a trade arrangement in which goods are shipped to a foreign buyer without guarantee of payment. Though this method is the riskiest, many firms that have a long-standing business relationship with the same over-seas firm, use this method. Needless to say, the key is to know your buyer and your buyer's country. You should use an open account when the buyer has a continuing need for the seller's product or service. Some experienced exporters say that they only deal in open accounts. But, they always preface that statement by saying that they have close relationships and have been doing business with those overseas clients for many years. An open account can be risky unless the buyer is of unques-tioned integrity and has withstood a thorough credit investiga-tion. The advantage of this method is its ease and convenience, but with open-account sales, you bear the burden of financing the shipment. Standard practice in many countries is to defer payment until the merchandise is sold, sometimes even longer. Therefore, among the forms of payment, open-account sales require the greatest amount of working capital. In addition, you bear the exchange risk if the sales are quoted in foreign cur-rency. Nevertheless, competitive pressures may force the use of this method.

Consignment. The seller (*consignor*) retains title to the goods during shipment and storage of the product in the ware-house or retail store. The consignee acts as a selling agent, selling the goods and remitting the net proceeds to the con-signor. Like open-account sales, consignment sales also can be risky and lend themselves only to certain kinds of merchandise. You should take great care in working out this contractual arrangement. Be sure you cover it with adequate risk insurance.

Bank Draft. Payments for many sales are arranged using one of many time-tested banking methods. Bills of exchange or bank drafts sight and time are useful under certain circumstances.

A *bank draft* is a check, drawn by a bank on another bank, used primarily where it is necessary for the customer to provide funds payable at a bank in some distant location.

Time (date) Draft. This draft is an order drawn by the exporter on the importer (customer), payable a certain number of days after "sight" (presentation) to the holder. Documents, such as negotiable bills of lading, insurance certificates, and commercial invoices, accompany the draft and are submitted through the exporter's bank for collection. When you present the draft to the importer at his bank, the importer acknowledges that the documents are acceptable and commits to pay by writing "Accepted" on the draft and signing it. The importer normally has 30 to 180 days, depending on the draft's term, to make payments to its bank for transmittal.

Sight Draft. This is similar to the time draft except that the importer's bank holds the documents until the importer releases the funds. Although this method costs less than the Letter of Credit (defined later), it has greater risk because the importer can refuse to honor the draft.

Bill of Lading A document that provides the terms of the contract between the shipper and the transportation company to move freight between stated points at a specified charge.

Commercial or Customs Invoice A bill for the goods from the seller to the buyer. It is one method used by governments to determine the value of the goods for customs valuation purposes.

At Sight Indicates that a negotiable instrument is to be paid upon presentation or demand.

Authority to Purchase. The Far East uses this method occasionally. The importer specifies a bank in the United States where the exporter can draw a documentary draft on the importer's bank. The problem with this method is that if the importer fails to pay the draft, the bank has "recourse" to the exporter for settlement. If an exporter consents to this method, it is suggested that the Authority to Purchase specify "without recourse" and so state it on the drafts.

The major risk with the time, sight, and authority-to-purchase methods is that the buyer can refuse to pay or to pick up the goods. The method of avoidance is to require cash against documents. Unfortunately, this method is slow because banks are slow in transferring funds. They want to use the *time float* (short-term investment of bank money) to make interest. Using a wire transfer can get around this.

Letters of Credit (L/C). Ideally, an exporter would deal only in cash, but in reality, few businesspeople initially are able or willing to do business under those terms. Because of the risk of nonpayment due to insolvency, bankruptcy, or other severe deterioration, procedures and documents have been developed which help to ensure that foreign buyers honor their agreements. The most common form of collection is payment against a *Letter of Credit* (L/C). The L/C is the time-tested method whereby an importer's bank guarantees that if all documents are presented in exact conformity with the terms of the L/C, they will pay the exporter. The procedure is not difficult to understand, and most cities have banks with people who are familiar with the L/C's mechanics.

This method is understood well by traders around the world; it is simple; and it is as good as your bank. Internationally, the term most often used is "documentary credits." They involve thousands of transactions and billions of dollars every day in every part of the world. They are operated almost always in accordance with the Uniform Customs and Practice for Documentary Credits of the International Chamber of Commerce, a code of practice which is recognized by banking communities in 156 countries. A *Guide to Documentary Operations*, which includes all of the standard forms, is available by writing to the ICC Publishing Corporation, Inc., 156 Fifth Ave., Suite 820, New York, NY 10010 or ICC Services S.A.R.L., 38 Cours Albert ler, 75008 PARIS, telephone 261-85-97 or telex 650770.

An L/C is a document issued by a bank at the importer's or buyer's request in favor of the seller. It promises to pay a specified amount of money upon receipt by the bank of certain documents, within a specified time. It is a universally-used method of achieving a commercially-acceptable compromise. Think of a Letter of Credit as an escrow account, like those used when buying a house. The amount in the escrow account depends on the relationship of the buyer and the buyer's bank.

Typically, if you don't already have an account, the bank

will require 100% collateral. With an account, the bank will establish a line of credit against that account. For instance, if you have $5000.00 in your account and the transaction is expected to cost $1000.00, your account will be reduced to $4000.00 and the line of credit established as $1000.00

Typical charges are as follows.

- To handle an import L/C: 1/4 of 1% of the transaction, with a minimum of $50.00 to $100.00.
  Amendments to the L/C might cost $40.00.
  Negotiations (=payments) of the L/C might cost $50.00.

- To handle the export L/C: 1/10 of 1% of the transaction with a minimum of $50–$65.
  Advising fees might be $45.00.

Sometimes when dealing in an open account, the exporter requires a "standby L/C". This statement means just what the name implies, the L/C is not to be executed unless payment is not made within the specified period, usually 30-60 days. Bank handling charges for standby letters of credit are usually higher than for a commercial (import) L/C.

Letters of Credit are payable at sight or on a time draft basis. Under a sight L/C, the issuing bank pays, with or without a draft, when satisfied that the presented documents conform with the forms. Under a time or acceptance L/C, once the associated draft is presented and found to be in exact conformity, the draft is stamped "accepted" and then can be negotiated as a "banker's acceptance" by the exporter, at a discount, to reflect the cost of money advanced against the draft.

Revocable credit means the document can be amended or cancelled at any time without prior warning or notification of the seller.

Irrevocable simply means that the terms of the document can be amended or cancelled only with the agreement of all parties thereto.

Confirmation means the United States bank guarantees payment by the foreign bank.

To: Importer's international bank
_____
                  Request to open documentary
                  credit (commercial letter of
                  credit and security agreement)

                  Date _____

     Please open for my/our account a documentary credit
(letter of credit) in accordance with the undermentioned
particulars.
     We agree that, except so far as otherwise expressly stated,
this credit will be subject to the Uniform Customs and
Practice for Documentary Credits, ICC Publication #290.

     We undertake to execute the Bank's usual form of
indemnity.

Type of Credit: Irrevocable, i.e., cannot be cancelled without
                            beneficiary's agreement.
                Revocable, i.e., subject to cancellation.
Method of Advice: [ ]   Airmail   [ ]   Cable, short
details   [ ]   Cable, full details.
Beneficiary's bank: _____

In favor of Beneficiary: Company name and address.

Amount or sum of:

Availability: Valid until_____in_____for negotiation/
                   date   place acceptance/payment.

This credit is available by drafts drawn at ____ sight/
accompanied by the required documents.

Documents
required: Invoice in three copies
           Full set clean "on board" bills of lading to order of
           shipper, blank endorsed. In case movement of goods

Fig. 4-1   An example of a request to open a Letter of Credit.

involves more than one mode, a "Combined Transport Document" should be called for.

Negotiable Marine and War risk insurance for % (usually 110%) of invoice value covering all risks.

Certificate of Inspection

Other
Documents: Certificate of origin issued by Chamber of Commerce in three copies.

Packing List

Quantity &
Description
of Goods

Price per unit:

Terms &
relative port
or place: C.I.F./C.&F./F.O.B./F.A.S./ _____
Place _____

Dispatch/
Shipment   From _____ to _____

Special
Instructions
(if any):

Fig. 4-1   (Cont.)

Once the buyer and the seller agree that they will use an L/C for payment, and they have worked out the conditions or contract, the buyer or importer applies for the L/C to his or her international bank. Figure 4-1 is an example of a letter of credit application.

Using the application as its guide, the bank issues a document of credit incorporating the terms agreed to by the parties. Figure 4-2 exemplifies a L/C.

Figure 4-3 shows the three phases of documentary credit, in their simplest form. In Phase I, your bank notifies the seller or the seller's bank that a credit has been issued. In Phase II, the seller then ships the goods and presents the documents to

Name of Issuing Bank	Documentary Credit No. _____
Place and date of issue	Place and date of expiration
Applicant	Amount
	Credit available with [ ] Payment [ ] Acceptance [ ] Negotiation
Shipment from _____ Shipment to _____	Against presentation of documents detailed herein [ ] Drawn on _____. Bank

Invoice in three copies

Full set clean "on board" bills of lading to order of shipper, blank endorsed. In case movement of goods involves more than one made, a "Combined Transport Document" should be called for.

Negotiable Marine and War risk insurance for _____ % (usually 110%) of invoice value covering all risks.

Certificate of Inspection

Certificate of origin issued by Chamber of Commerce in three copies.

Packing List

Documents to be presented within _____ days after date of issuance of the shipping document(s) but within the validity of the credit.

We hereby issue this Documentary Credit in your favor.

Issuing Bank

Fig. 4-2   A sample Letter of Credit.

the bank, at which time, the seller is paid. Phase III is the "settlement" phase, wherein, the documents are then transferred to the buyer's bank, whereupon the buyer pays the bank any remaining money in exchange for the documents. Thus, on

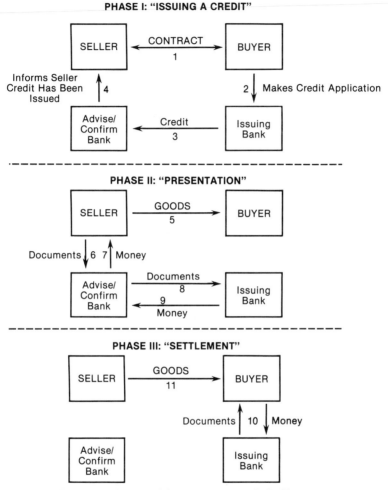

Fig. 4-3   The three phases of documentary credit (L/C).

arrival of the goods, the buyer or importer has the proper documents for entry.

Cash in Advance. This collection method is the most desirable, but just as in America, the foreign buyer usually objects to tying up capital. On the grounds that seeing the merchandise is the best insurance, most foreign businessmen try not to pay until they actually receive the goods. Furthermore, the buyer might resent the implication that he or she might not be creditworthy.

Table 4-1 summarizes and compares the various methods

Table 4-1 Payment Methods

(In order of decreasing risk to exporter and increasing risk to importer)

Method	Goods available to buyers	Usual time of payment	Exporter risk	Importer risk
Open account	Before payment	As agreed	Most Relies on importer to pay account	Least
Consign- ment	Before payment	After sold	Maximum Exporter retains title	Minor inventory cost
Time draft	Before payment	On maturity of draft	High Relies on importer to pay draft	Minimal check of quantity/ quality
Sight draft	After payment	On presenting draft to importer	If unpaid goods are returned/ disposed	Little if inspection report rq'd
Authority to Purchase	After payment	On presenting draft	Be careful of recourse	Little if inspection report rq'd
Letter of Credit	After payment	When documents are available after shipment	None	None if inspection report rq'd
Cash	After payment	Before shipment	Least	Most

of payment in order of decreasing risk to the exporter and increasing risk to the importer.

Avoiding Bad Credit

Pick your customer carefully. Just as in the domestic American market, bad debts are avoided more easily than rectified.

If there are payment problems, keep communicating and working with the firm until you have settled the matter. Even the most valued customers have financial problems from time to time. If nothing else works, request that the Department of Commerce or the International Chamber of Commerce begin arbitration on your behalf.

Information that is current and accurate is the food for good financing decisions. Basically, two types of international credit information exists: (1) the ability and willingness of importing firms to make payment, and (2) the ability and willingness of foreign countries to allow payment in a convertible currency.

Following are several ways to obtain credit information about companies and their countries:

Information about United States Firms.

• Commercial Banks

• Commercial credit services, such as Dun and Bradstreet

• Trade Associations

Information about Foreign Firms.

• National Association of Credit Management (NACM)

• Foreign credit specialists in the credit departments of exporting companies

• Commercial banks, which check buyer credit through their foreign branches and correspondents

• Commercial credit reporting services, such as Dun and Bradstreet

• Consultations with the EXIMBANK and the Foreign Credit Insurance Association (FCIA)

• The United States Commerce Department's World Trade Directory Reports

Information about Foreign Countries.

• World Bank

• Chase World Information Corporation

• The Magazine Institutional Investor

• National Association of Credit Management (NACM)

Insurance

In addition to the various methods of avoiding nonpayment, insurance against marine, commercial, and political risk also is available.

Avoiding Shipping Risks. Marine cargo insurance is an essential business tool for import/export. Generally, you purchase coverage on a warehouse-to-warehouse basis (i.e. from the sender's factory to the receiver's platform). Coverage usually ceases a specific number of days after the ship or plane is unloaded. You purchase policies on a per shipment or "blanket" basis. Freight forwarders usually have a blanket policy to cover clients who do not have their own policy. Most insurance companies base cargo insurance on the value of all charges of the shipment, including freight handling, etc., plus 10% to cover unseen contingencies. Rates vary according to product, client's track record, destination, and shipping method.

Ocean cargo insurance costs about $.50 to $1.50 per $100.00 of invoice value. Air cargo is usually about 25% to 30% less.

Avoiding Political Risk. No two national export credit systems are identical. However, there are similarities, the greatest of which is the universal involvement of government through the export credit agency concerned and of the commercial banking sector in the workings of the system.

In the United States, the Export-Import Bank (EXIM-BANK) serves by providing credit support in the form of loans, guarantees, and insurance. EXIMBANK cooperates with commercial United States and foreign banks in providing a number of arrangements to help United States exporters offer credit guarantees to commercial banks that finance export sales. Through the Overseas Private Investment Corporation (OPIC) and the Foreign Credit Insurance Association (FCIA), EXIM-BANK also provides insurance to United States exporters, enabling them to extend credit terms to their overseas buyers. Private insurers cover the normal commercial credit risks; EXIMBANK assumes all liability for political risk.

The programs available through OPIC and FCIA are advertised well and easily are available. Commercial banks are essentially intermediaries to the EXIMBANK for export guarantees on loans (beginning at loans up to 1 year and ending at loans of up to 10-15 years). FCIA offers insurance in two basic maturities: (1) short-term policy of up to 180 days, (2) a medium-term policy from 181 days up to 5 years; or you might obtain a combination policy of those maturities. FCIA also has a master policy providing *blanket protection* (one policy designed to provide coverage for all the exporter's sales to overseas buyers).

Avoiding Foreign Exchange Risk. When the dollar is strong—as strong as it was in the early 1980s—traders prefer to deal in the dollar. When the opposite is true, traders begin to deal in other currencies. The dollar is as good as gold. It is a politically-stable currency, and is traded internationally. It has become the vehicle currency for most international transactions because it is the world's major trading currency.

So long as American exporters deal only in the dollar, there is no foreign exchange risk. However, the strength and popularity of currencies is cyclic, and the dollar is not always the leader. Often, an exporter is faced with the prospect of pricing products or services in currencies other than United States dollars. Importers must buy foreign currency to pay for products and services from risk-avoiding foreign suppliers demanding payment in their own currency. In the current era of floating exchange rates, there are risks due to exposure whenever there are cash flows denominated in foreign currencies.

Successfully managing currency risk is imperative. No longer can an importer/exporter speculate by doing nothing, then pass their foreign exchange losses on to customers in the form of higher prices. The best business decision for an importer/exporter is to hedge or cover in the forward market when there is risk of exposure. To do otherwise is to be a speculator, not a businessperson. Use the forward rate for the date on which payment is required. This rate avoids all foreign exchange risk, is simple, and is reasonably inexpensive. The cost of a forward contract is small—the difference between the cost of the *spot market* (today's cost of money) and the cost of the forward market. Major international banks and brokerage houses can help you arrange a foreign-exchange forward contract. Spot and forward markets are quoted daily in the *Wall Street Journal*.

Exposure is the effect on a firm or an individual if there is a change on exchange rates.

Hedging or covering is the use of the forward foreign exchange market to avoid foreign currency risk.

The forward or *future exchange rate* is the rate that is contracted today for the delivery of a currency at a specified date in the future, at a price agreed upon today.

Agency/Distributor Agreements

Earlier, in chapter 3, I discussed your relationship with overseas distributors. A manufacturer or importer/exporter will seldom agree to meet all of a distributor's conditions. Most terms are negotiable, and a firm that is not internationally known might have to grant more demands than others in a more favorable position. The following five tips might help to avoid risk in doing business with distributors:

1. **Put the agency agreement in writing.** The rights and obligations resulting from a written agreement require no extraneous proof and are all that is necessary to record or prove the terms of a contract in most countries.

2. **Set forth the benefit to both parties in the agreement.** Well-balanced agreements should not place an excess of profitless burden on one of the parties. Performance of the agreement might be impossible to enforce against a party who has no apparent benefit from it.

3. **Give clear definition and meaning to all contract terms**. Many English terms that are spelled similarly in the foreign language have entirely different meanings. Require that the English version prevail when there is doubt. To avoid conflict use INCOTERMS.

4. **Expressly state the rights and obligations of the parties.** The agency contract should contain a description of the rights and duties of each party, the nature and duration of the relationship, and the reasons for which the agreement might be terminated.

5. **Specify a jurisdictional clause.** If local laws will allow, specify in the contract the jurisdiction to handle any legal disputes that might arise. Where possible, use arbitration. Basic arbitration rules and principles are generally the same anywhere. Clauses in the contract should contain identification of the arbitration body or forum. You can obtain model arbitration clauses from the American Arbitration Association, 140 West 51st Street, New York, NY 10020 or the International Chamber of Commerce, 1212 Avenue of the Americas, New York, NY 10036.

Physical Distribution (Shipping and Packing)

Physical distribution, sometimes referred to as logistics, is the means by which goods are moved from the manufacturer in one country to the customer in another. This section discusses two vital aspects for which the importer/exporter should have an appreciation: shipping and packing.

Shipping. The importer/exporter can arrange directly land, ocean, and air shipments of international cargo. You handle inland transportation much the same as a domestic transaction, except that you must add certain export marks to the standard information shown on a domestic bill of lading. Also include instructions to the inland carrier to notify the ocean or air carrier.

Water Transportation. Three types of ocean service are available: conference lines, independent lines, and tramp vessels. An *ocean conference* is an association of ocean carriers that have joined together to establish common rates and shipping conditions. Conferences have two rates: the regular tariff and a lower, contract rate. You can obtain the contract rate if you sign a contract to use conference vessels exclusively during the contract period. *Independent lines* accept bookings from all shippers contingent on the availability of space and are often less expensive than conference rates. An independent usually quotes rates about 10% lower than a conference carrier in situations where the two are in competition. *Tramp vessels* usually carry only bulk cargoes and do not follow an established schedule; rather they operate on charters.

Regardless of the type carrier you use, the carrier will issue a booking contract, which reserves space on a specific ship. Unless you cancel in advance, you might be required to pay, even if your cargo doesn't make the sailing. You must be insured with ocean marine insurance. An insurance broker or your freight forwarder can arrange this for you.

Marine Insurance An insurance that will compensate the owner of goods transported on the seas in the event of loss that would not be legally recovered from the carrier. It also covers air shipments.

Air Transportation. Air freight continues to grow as a popular and competitive method for international cargoes. The growth has been facilitated by innovation in the cargo industry. Air carriers have excellent capacity, use very efficient loading and unloading equipment, and handle standardized containers. The advantages are (a) the speed of delivery, which gets perishable cargoes to the place of destination in prime condition, (b) the ability to respond to unpredictable product demands, and (c) the rapid movement of repair parts.

Air freight moves under a general cargo rate or a commodity rate. A special unit load rate is available when using approved air shipping containers.

Land Transportation. Transportation over land in the United States has become less regulated and, therefore, more competitive and efficient. Road and rail serve two of the largest United States import/export markets—Canada and Mexico. For all the rest, American importers and exporters look primarily to land transportation to move their goods to the nearest port of departure or as one leg of a sea, land, or air combination often referred to as *intermodalism.*

Intermodalism: The movement of international shipments via container using sequential transportation methods is the system of the future. The concept makes use of the most efficient and cost effective methods to move goods.

Load centering: This concept stimulated the sophistication of today's intermodal world. As ships grew to hold more containers, they became more expensive to operate. One way to reduce costs was to hold down the number of port calls. In order to fill the ships at fewer ports, the cargo must be funneled into these load centers. The simplification and organization of movements of cargo has become the "fair haired" child of transportation specialists. An entirely new set of terms have developed around the concept.

A *micro-bridge* is the routing of a container to or from anywhere in the United States to or from any port. A *minibridge* moves a container that originates or terminates in a United States port other than the one where it enters or leaves the country. A *land bridge* off-loads a container at any United States port, ships it cross-country by rail, then reloads aboard a vessel for final movement to a foreign destination. *RO/RO* refers to the roll on/roll off capability of containerized cargo, which is the foundation of intermodalism.

An example of intermodalism might be a container of goods originating in Europe but destined for Japan. It could be rolled off a ship by truck then onto a train in Newport News, Virginia (RO/RO), where it would be joined by another container trucked in from Florida, (minibridge) also destined for Japan. The containers would then be moved across the United States (land bridge), then rolled off the train and onto a ship in Long Beach which would complete the movement to Tokyo. Figure 4-4 illustrates the intermodal concept.

If the details of transportation and all the "new fangled" ideas are not for you, then see your nearest freight forwarder (explained in chapter 5).

Packaging and Marking for Overseas Shipment. Whether importing or exporting, your product(s) must travel thousands of miles in an undamaged condition. Your package must protect against breakage, dampeners, careless storage, rough handling, thieves, and weather. Insurance might cover the loss, but lost time and the ill will of your overseas trading partner is a high price to pay. Estimates show that proper packaging and marking could prevent as much as 70% of all cargo loss.

An excellent source on all aspects of packing and packaging is *Modern Packaging Encyclopedia* (Annual), McGraw-Hill, NY.

Breakage. Ocean shipments often are loaded aboard by stevedores using forklifts, slings, nets, and conveyors. During the voyage, rough water and storms can cause loads to shift and sometimes crash into other containers. Even small packages sent through the mails can be squeezed, thrown, or crushed.

Assume the worst when packaging for overseas delivery. Use stronger and heavier materials than for domestic shipments. On the other hand, don't overpack—you pay by weight and volume. For large ocean shipments, consider standardized containers that can be transferred from truck or rail car without opening.

Pilferage (Theft). Use strapping and seals and avoid trademarks or content descriptions.

Moisture and Weather. The heat and humidity of the tropics as well as rainstorms and rough weather at sea can cause moisture to seep into the holds of a ship. From that moisture comes fungal growths, sweat, and rust. Waterproofing your shipment is essential for most ocean shipments. Consider plastic shrink-wrap or waterproof inner liners, and coat any exposed metal parts with grease or other rust inhibitors.

Marking (Labeling). Foreign customers have their needs, shippers have theirs, and terminal operators have theirs. Each will specify certain marks (port, customer identification code, package numbers, and number of packages) to appear on shipments. You also can specify other markings, such as weight,

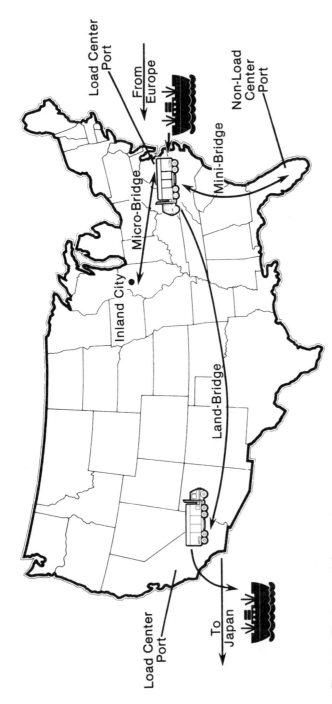

Fig. 4-4   The intermodal concept.

dimensions, and regulations that facilitate clearing through customs. Figure 4-5 is a sample of markings.

Checklist for Shipping

☑ Write your customer's name and address or shipping code on the package.

☑ Use black, waterproof ink for the stencils.

☑ Include port of exit and port of entry on your label.

☑ Place package and case number on container.

☑ Include dimensions (inches and metric).

☑ Mark exports, "Made in U.S.A." to get through customs in most foreign countries.

☑ Express gross and net weight in pounds and/or kilograms.

☑ Use cautionary markings such as "this side up" or "handle with care" in both languages.

☑ Don't use brand names or advertising slogans on packages.

☑ Make sure any shipments that carry explosives or volatile liquids conform to local law and international agreements.

DOCUMENTATION

"Attention to detail" is the byword when preparing documentation. The naive pass it off as a by-product of the transaction, but the experienced trader knows that inattention detains shipments on the pier for weeks. As ex-Yankee baseball player Yogi Berra once said, "It ain't over 'til it's over," and that's the way it is in international trade. The exporter doesn't get his or her money and the importer doesn't get his or her goods unless the paperwork is complete and accurate! Therefore, be attentive to detail!!

Basically, documentation falls into two categories: shipping and collecting.

Shipping

Shipping documents permit an export cargo to be moved through customs, loaded aboard a carrier, and shipped to its foreign destination. These documents are:

• Export licenses

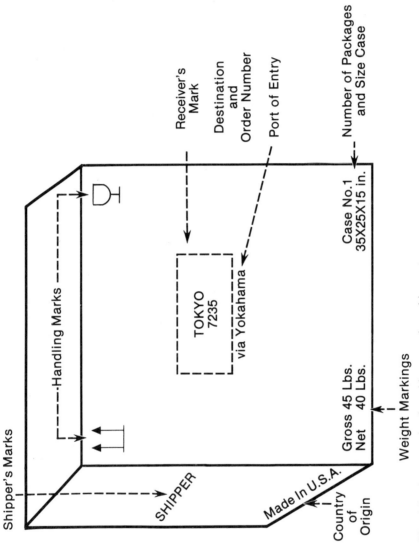

Fig. 4-5   An example of markings used on shipments.

- Packing lists
- Bills of lading
- Export declarations

Collection

Collection documents are those needed for submission to the importer (in the case of a draft) or to the importer's bank (in the case of an L/C) in order to receive payment. These documents are:

- Commercial invoices
- Consular invoices
- Certificates of origin
- Inspection certificates
- Bills of lading

When endorsed by the shipper, you can use the bill of lading for sight draft or for L/C shipments. Other documents sometimes required for collection are manufacturing and insurance certificates and dock or warehouse receipts. Keep in mind that customhouse brokers and freight forwarders are specialists in documentation as well as physical distribution.

Collection The procedure whereby a bank collects money for a seller against a draft drawn on a buyer abroad, usually through a correspondent bank.

The Documents

This section describes the various documents in detail and provides samples of each.

Certificate of Origin

The *Certificate of Origin* is a document that certifies to the buyer the country in which the goods were produced. A recognized Chamber of Commerce usually performs the certificate of the origin of merchandise. Some countries require a separate certificate, sometimes countersigned by a chamber of commerce and possibly even visaed by their resident consul at the port of export. These statements are required to indicate preferential rates of import duties such as "most favored nation." Often, as little as 35% of a nation's materials and/or labor can qualify it for favorable duties. Some nations require special forms, while others accept a certification on the shipper's own letterhead. See Figure 4-6 for an example of a Certificate of Origin.

Checklist for Certificates of Origin

☑ The letter or form should originate from the address of the manufacturer of the product.

☑ A responsible and knowledgeable person within the manufacturing company (i.e., an officer of the corporation) must sign the letter.

☑ The letter or form will not be accepted if it is from an outside sales office or distributor, and a salesperson is not permitted to sign it.

☑ The letter should state clearly where the product in question was manufactured.

Commercial Invoice

The commercial invoice is a bill that conforms in all respects to the agreement between importer and exporter. It could have the exact terms of the pro forma invoice first offered in response to a quotation, or it could differ in those terms that were the result of final negotiations. In any case, there should be no surprises for the importer. The commercial invoice should (a) itemize the merchandise by price per unit and any charges paid by the buyer, and (b) specify the terms of payment and any marks or numbers on the packages. See Figure 4-7.

Consular Invoice

This invoice is not required by all countries. You obtain it from the commercial attache or through the consular office of the country in the port of export. When required, it is in addition to a commercial invoice and must conform in every respect to that document as well as the bill of lading and any insurance documents. Its purpose is to allow clearance of your shipment into the country that requires it. See Figure 4-8.

Commercial Attache The commercial expert on the diplomatic staff of his country's embassy or large consulate in a foreign country.

Our Company, Inc.

Home Town, Wherever

Date _____

Your Company

Home Town, Wherever

Point of Origin Declaration

For the purpose of positively identifying certain

components as

being manufactured in _____ and there-
(Country)
fore qualifying for entry under _____.
(Tariff code identification)
Component(s) description: _____

_____.

Part number: _____

_____.

The manufacturer _____ warrants and

represents that the articles supplied to _____

_____
(Company)
and described above are articles of _____.

(Country)
The articles were manufactured at _____
(Address of location of plant)

_____.

_____
Authorized signature and date

_____
Title

Fig. 4-6   An example of a certificate of origin.

XYZ Foreign, Co.
2A1 Moon River
Yokohama, Japan

Purchase Order:
Invoice Number: 00012
Invoice Date:

Sold To: Our Company, Inc.   Ship To: Our Company, Inc.
　　　　Hometown, U.S.A.   Hometown, U.S.A.

Forwarding Agent:

Via: Country of Origin: Japan

QUANTITY	PART NO.	DESCRIPTION	PRICE EACH	TOTAL PRICE
10	A2Z	Machines	$100.00	$1,000.00

Inland freight, export packing & forwarding fees $ 100.00

Free alongside (F.A.S.) Yokohama $1,100.00
Estimated ocean freight $ 100.00
Estimated marine insurance $ 50.00

Packed in 10 crates, 100 cubic feet
Gross weight 1000 lbs.
Net   weight 900 lbs.
Payment terms: Confirmed irrevocable letter of credit
confirmed by a U.S. bank. Shipment to be made two (2)
weeks after receipt of firm order.
Additional conditions of sale: XYZ, Foreign Co. to provide:
Certificate of Origin
Consular Invoice
Certificate of Manufacture
Insurance Certificate
Inspection Certificate

Fig. 4-7   A commercial invoice.

Certificate of Manufacture

This document certifies that the goods ordered by the
importer have been produced and are ready for shipment. For
example it might be used in those cases when the manufacturer
has moved ahead in production with only a down payment, thus

FACTURA COMERCIAL

No. de la Factura.............
(Commercial Invoice #)

Lugar (Ciudad)................
Place (City)

Fecha: Día........
Date: Day

Mes........
Mo.

Año.........
Year

INTERVIENEN	Nombre de la Cía. o del Agente autorizado	DOMICILIO (Address)		
		Calle (Street)	Número (No.)	Ciudad (City)	Tel. (Phone)
Vendedor o rémitente (Seller or shipper)					
Comprador (Buyer)					
Consig. a Destinatario (Consigned to)					
Agente o Gestor Agent-Broker					

Lugar y Puerto de Embarque Port of Loading	Lugar y Puerto de Destino Port of Unloading	Fecha de Embarque Date of Shipment	Nombre del Buque o Cía. Aérea Transp. Vessel/Airline Name

CONDICIONES DE VENTA: FOB - CIF   SEGURO (Insurance): ....

Cantidad y Número de Bultos	PESO		Detalle descriptivo de la mercadería, indicando marca, lugar de fabricación, clase o tipo del producto, series, numeros, etc. y cualquier otra información adicional relacionada. (Denomination and details of each article: quantity, quality, measure, merch. origin, etc.)	Precio de la Mercadería (Merchandise Price)
	Kilogramos	Libras		

Fig. 4-8   An example of a Consular Invoice.

Importe mercad. ...U$S
Merch. Price

Transporte ....U$S

Otros (other) ......U$S

SUB-TOTAL ....U$S

Tasa Consular, Fee U$S

IMPORTE TOTAL U$S

The...

A recognized Chamber of Commerce under the laws or the State of California has examined the manufacturer's invoice or shipper affidavit concerning the origin of the merchandise and according to the best of its knowledge and belief, finds that the products named originated in the United States of North America.

Authorized Officer........................... Date...............

Espacio para Certificacion Consular

Fig. 4-8 Continued

El agente autorizado que firma la presente, declara bajo juramento que todos los datos declarados en la presente factura, son exactos y verdaderos y que los precios pagados o por pagarse, son los reales y convenidos, que no existe convenio o arreglo alguno que permita la alteración o modificación de éstos, ni tampoco de su cantidad o calidad.

Firma del Agente, Vendedor o
Despachante autorizado. Fecha.: ....

FACTURA COMERCIAL No.

Certifico que la firma que aparece en este

documento y dice ....

....
es auténtica y pertenece al funcionario des-

cripto.

Los Angeles, Calif. ....

Número de orden ....

No. del arancel ....

Der. percib. U$S. ....

Depositado en el Banco

allowing the importer to avoid allocation of the full amount too far in advance. Generally, invoices and packing lists are forwarded to the importer with the certificate of manufacture. See Figure 4-9.

Export Licenses

Export licensing procedures are described in detail in chapter 5 as one of the six topics unique to exporting. These licenses are of two basic varieties: general and validated. Validated licenses require careful attention because they apply to products that the United States government wants to control closely for strategic or economic reasons. The Export Administration regulations set forth all licensing requirements for commodities under the jurisdiction of the Office of Export Administration (OEA), International Trade Administration. Once it has been determined that a license is needed, the form "Application for

---

DATE:

REFERENCE: ACCOUNT NAME & ADDRESS
            PURCHASE ORDER NO. AND/OR
            CONTRACT NO.

BANK NAME AND LETTER OF CREDIT NO:

MERCHANDISE DESCRIPTION:

CERTIFICATE OF RECENT MANUFACTURE

WE HEREBY CERTIFY THAT THE HEREIN DESCRIBED MERCHANDISE IS OF RECENT MANUFACTURE IN THIS CASE NOT OLDER THAN _____ YEAR(S) FROM THIS DATE.

NAME AND ADDRESS OF MANUFACTURER:

BY: _____
                    (original signature)

Fig. 4-9   An example of a Certificate of Manufacture.

Export License" must be prepared and submitted to the OEA. See Figure 5-1 in chapter 5.

Insurance Certificates

This document provides evidence of coverage and might be a stipulation of a contract, purchase order, or commercial invoice in order to receive payment. These certificates indicate the type and amount of coverage and identify the merchandise in terms of packages and identifying marks. You should make certain that the information on this certificate agrees exactly with invoices and bills of lading. See Figure 4-10.

Inspection Certificates

This document protects the importer against fraud, error, or quality performance. An independent firm usually conducts the inspection, but sometimes the shipper performs it. Terms of a letter of credit often require an affidavit that certifies the inspection. For example, a Taiwanese firm wanted to import used diesel generators from the United States. That company insisted that an independent engineer certify satisfactory operation of each generator, at specifications, prior to shipment. See Figure 4-11.

Packing Lists

A packing list accompanies the shipment and describes the cargo in detail. It includes the shipper, the consignee, measurements, serial numbers, weights, and any other data peculiar to the shipment. When correctly completed, it is placed in a waterproof bag or envelope and attached with the words: "Packing List Enclosed." See Figure 4-12.

Shippers Export Declaration

The exporter or freight forwarder for the United States government prepares the export declaration. All exports in excess of $1000.00 require this form. It provides statistical information to the Bureau of Census and indicates the proper authorization to export. The document requires complete information about the shipment, including description, value, net and gross weights, and relevant license information, thus closing the licensing information loop back to the OEA. See Figure 4-13.

No. 573951

CERTIFICATE OF MARINE INSURANCE

International Cargo & Surety Insurance Company

*$ _____
(sum insured)

This is to Certify, That on the _____ day of _____ 19 ___ , this Company

insured under Policy No. _____ made for

for the sum of _____ Dollars,

on

*(Amounts in excess of $1,000,000.00 cannot be insured under this Certificate)

Valued at sum insured. Shipped on board the S/S or M/S

at and from _____ and/or following
(Initial Point of Shipment)   steamer or steamers

_____ , via _____
(Port of Places of Destination)   (Port of Shipment)

to _____ and it is understood and agreed, that in case of loss, the same

is payable to the order of

conveys the right of collecting any such loss as fully as if the property were covered by a special policy direct to the holder hereof, on surrender of the Certificate which any liability for unpaid premiums. This certificate is issued subject to the standard International Cargo & Surety Insurance Company open cargo policy, which is incorporated herein by reference, to the extent that any terms or conditions in this certificate are inconsistent with the standard policy, the standard policy shall govern the rights and duties of all parties subject to the contract of insurance. Copies of the standard policy are available, upon request, from International Cargo & Surety Insurance Company, 1501 Woodfield Road, Schaumburg, Illinois 60173.

SPECIAL CONDITIONS   MARKS & NUMBERS

Merchandise shipped with an UNDER DECK bill of lading insured—
Against all risks of physical loss or damage from any external cause, irrespective of percentage, excepting those excluded by the F.C. & S and S.R. & C.C. Warranties, arising during transportation between the points of shipment and of destination named herein.

SCHEDULE B CODE (commodity)	SCHEDULE C-E CODE (country)

ON DECK SHIPMENTS (with an ON DECK bill of lading) and/or shipments of used merchandise insured:
Warranted free of particular average unless caused by the vessel being stranded, sunk, burnt, on fire or in collision, but including risk of jettison and/or washing overboard, irrespective of percentage.

TERMS AND CONDITIONS—SEE ALSO BACK HEREOF

WAREHOUSE TO WAREHOUSE: This insurance attaches from the time the goods leave the Warehouse and/or Store at the place named in the Policy for the commencement of the transit and continues during the ordinary course of transit, including customary transhipment if any, until the goods are discharged overside from the overseas vessel at the final port. Thereafter the insurance continues whilst the goods are in transit and/or awaiting transit until delivered to final warehouse at the destination named in the Policy or until the expiry of 15 days (or 30 days if the destination to which the goods are insured is outside the limits of the port) whichever shall first occur. The time limits referred to above to be reckoned from midnight of the day on which the discharge overside of the goods hereby insured from the overseas vessel is completed. Held covered at a premium to be arranged in the event of transhipment, if any, other than as above and/or in the event of delay in excess of the above time limits arising from circumstances beyond the control of the Assured.

Fig. 4-10   An example of a Certificate of Marine Insurance.

NOTE – IT IS NECESSARY FOR THE ASSURED TO GIVE PROMPT NOTICE TO THESE ASSURERS WHEN THEY BECOME AWARE OF AN EVENT FOR WHICH THEY ARE "HELD COVERED" UNDER THIS POLICY AND THE RIGHT TO SUCH COVER IS DEPENDENT ON COMPLIANCE WITH THIS OBLIGATION.

PERILS CLAUSE: Touching the adventures and perils which this Company is contented to bear, and takes upon itself, they are of the seas, fires, assailing thieves, jettisons, barratry of the master and mariners, and all other like perils, losses and misfortunes (illicit or contraband trade excepted in all cases), that have or shall come to the hurt, detriment or damage of the said goods and merchandise, or any part thereof.

SHORE CLAUSE: Where this insurance by its terms covers while on docks, wharves or elsewhere on shore, and/or during land transportation, it shall include the risks of collision, derailment, overturning or other accident to the conveyance, fire, lightning, sprinkler leakage, cyclones, hurricanes, earthquakes, floods (meaning the rising of navigable waters), and/or collapse or subsidence of docks or wharves, even though the insurance be otherwise F.P.A.

BOTH TO BLAME CLAUSE: Where goods are shipped under a Bill of Lading containing the so-called "Both to Blame Collision" Clause, these Assurers agree as to all losses covered by this insurance, to indemnify the Assured for this Policy's proportion of any amount (not exceeding the amount insured) which the Assured may be legally bound to pay to the shipowners under such clause. In the event that such liability is asserted the Assured agree to notify these Assurers who shall have the right at their own cost and expense to defend the Assured against such claim.

MACHINERY CLAUSE: When the property insured under this Policy includes a machine consisting when complete for sale or use of several parts, then in case of loss or damage covered by this insurance to any part of such machine, these Assurers shall be liable only for the proportion of the insured value of the part lost or damaged, or at the Assured's option, for the cost and expense, including labor and forwarding charges, of replacing or repairing the lost or damaged part; but in no event shall these Assurers be liable for more than the insured value of the complete machine.

LABELS CLAUSE: In case of damage affecting labels, capsules or wrappers, these Assurers, if liable therefor under the terms of this policy, shall not be liable for more than an amount sufficient to pay the cost of new labels, capsules or wrappers, and the cost of reconditioning the goods, but in no event shall these Assurers be liable for more than the insured value of the damaged merchandise.

DELAY CLAUSE: Warranted free of claim for loss of market or for loss, damage or deterioration arising from delay, whether caused by a peril insured against or otherwise, unless expressly assumed in writing hereon.

AMERICAN INSTITUTE CLAUSES: This insurance, in addition to the foregoing, is also subject to the following American Institute Cargo Clauses, current forms:

1. CRAFT, ETC.
2. DEVIATION
3. WAREHOUSING & FORWARDING CHARGES.
   PACKAGES TOTALLY LOST LOADING, ETC.
4. GENERAL AVERAGE
5. EXPLOSION
6. BILL OF LADING, ETC.
7. MARINE EXTENSION CLAUSES
8. INCHMAREE
9. CONSTRUCTIVE TOTAL LOSS
10. CARRIER
11. S.R. & C. C. ENDORSEMENT
12. **WAR RISK INSURANCE**
13. **SOUTH AMERICA 60 DAY CLAUSE**

PARAMOUNT WARRANTIES: THE FOLLOWING WARRANTIES SHALL BE PARAMOUNT AND SHALL NOT BE MODIFIED OR SUPERSEDED BY ANY OTHER PROVISION INCLUDED HEREIN OR STAMPED OR ENDORSED HEREON UNLESS SUCH OTHER PROVISION REFERS SPECIFICALLY TO THE RISKS EXCLUDED BY THESE WARRANTIES AND EXPRESSLY ASSUMES THE SAID RISKS:

F.C. & S. (a) Notwithstanding anything herein contained to the contrary, this insurance is warranted free from capture, seizure, arrest, restraint, detainment, confiscation, preemption, requisition or nationalization, and the consequences thereof or any attempt thereat, whether in time of peace or war and whether lawful or otherwise; also warranted free, whether in time of peace or war, from all loss, damage or expense caused by any weapon of war employing atomic or nuclear fission and/or fusion or other reaction or radioactive force or matter or by any mine or torpedo also warranted free from all consequences of hostilities or warlike operations (whether there be a declaration of war or not), but this warranty shall not exclude collision or contact with aircraft, rockets or similar missiles or with any fixed or floating object (other than a mine or torpedo), stranding, heavy weather, fire or explosion unless caused directly (and independently of the nature of the voyage or service which the vessel concerned or, in the case of a collision, any other vessel involved therein, is performing) by a hostile act by or against a belligerent power; and for the purposes of this warranty "power" includes any authority maintaining naval, military or air forces in association with a power.

Further warranted free from the consequences of civil war, revolution, rebellion, insurrection, or civil strife arising therefrom, or piracy.

S. R. & C. C. (b) Warranted free of loss or damage caused by or resulting from strikes, lockouts, labor disturbances, riots, civil commotions or the acts of any person or persons taking part in any such occurrence or disorder.

This Certificate is issued in Original and Duplicate, one of which being accomplished the other to stand null and void. To support a claim local Revenue Laws may require this certificate to be stamped.

Not transferable unless countersigned

Countersigned _____

President   Kenneth J. Brown

                    Secretary

SAMPLE   ORIGINAL

Fig. 4-10. Continued

```
DATE:

REFERENCE:    ACCOUNT NAME & ADDRESS
              PURCHASE ORDER NO. AND/OR
              CONTRACT NO.

BANK NAME AND LETTER OF CREDIT NO.

MERCHANDISE DESCRIPTION:


              INSPECTION CERTIFICATE

WE HEREBY CERTIFY THAT THE HEREIN DESCRIBED
MERCHANDISE HAS BEEN INSPECTED AND FOUND TO
BE OF HIGHEST QUALITY AND IN GOOD WORKING
ORDER.



              PORTER INTERNATIONAL INC.

              BY: _____
```

Fig. 4-11   An example of an Inspection Certificate.

Bills of Lading

A *bill of lading* is a contract between the owner of the goods (exporter) and the carrier. It is evidence that the shipment has been made and is your receipt for the goods that have been shipped. Figure 4-14 is a Bill of Lading for an air carrier, called an Air Waybill. Figure 4-15 shows an ocean bill of lading.

Straight Bills of Lading. These forms are nonnegotiable bills that consign the goods to an importer or other party named on the document. Once consummated, the seller and/or the seller's bank loses title control because the goods will be delivered to anyone who can be identified as the consignee.

Order Bill of Lading. This form is a negotiable bill; that is, unlike the "straight" bill, it represents the title to the goods in transit and the original copy must be endorsed before it is presented to the bank for collection. In other words, the "order" bill can be used as collateral in financing—as documentation to discount or sell a draft. L/C transactions specify to whom the

To: Your Company   Date: _____
    2A1 Moon River
    Yokohama, Japan

Gentlemen:

Under your order No. <u>123</u>   the material listed below was shipped <u>1/1/88</u>   via   <u>Truck and vessel</u>

To: <u>Yokohama</u>

Via:

Shipment Consists of: Marks:

___ Cases ___ Packages   Your Company, Ltd.
                       2A1 Moon River
___ Crates ___ Cartons   Yokohama, Japan

___ Bbls ___ Drums   Made in U.S.A.

___ Reels   # 7235

Package Number	Weights (Lbs or Kilos)		Dimensions			Quality	Contents
	Gross	Legal Net	Ht.	Wth.	Lth.		
7235	45	40	35	25	15		Toys

Fig. 4-12 A sample packing list.

endorsement is to be made. Typically, they are made "in blank," or to the order of a third party, a bank, or a broker.

    Air bills of lading are usually "straight" (i.e., nonnegotiable). Ocean shipping companies can issue "straight" or "to order."

U.S. DEPARTMENT OF COMMERCE — BUREAU OF THE CENSUS — INTERNATIONAL TRADE ADMINISTRATION

SHIPPER'S EXPORT DECLARATION

FORM **7525-V** (3-19-85)

OMB No. 0607-0018

1a. EXPORTER *(Name and address including ZIP code)*

ZIP CODE

2. DATE OF EXPORTATION

3. BILL OF LADING/AIR WAYBILL NO.

b. EXPORTER EIN NO.

c. PARTIES TO TRANSACTION
☐ Related   ☐ Non-related

4a. ULTIMATE CONSIGNEE

b. INTERMEDIATE CONSIGNEE

NONE

5. FORWARDING AGENT

Porter International, Inc.
P.O. Box 41-A
San Ysidro, California 92173

6. POINT (STATE) OF ORIGIN OR FTZ NO.

7. COUNTRY OF ULTIMATE DESTINATION

MEXICO

8. LOADING PIER/TERMINAL

9. MODE OF TRANSPORT *(Specify)*

TRUCK

10. EXPORTING CARRIER

Truck Lic.:

11. PORT OF EXPORT

San Diego, (S.Y.), California

12. FOREIGN PORT OF UNLOADING

13. CONTAINERIZED *(Vessel only)*
☐ Yes   ☐ No

Fig. 4-13   A sample Shipper's Export Declaration.

VALUE (U.S. dollars, omit cents) *(Selling price or cost if not sold)* (20)

14. SCHEDULE B DESCRIPTION OF COMMODITIES, *(Use columns 15 — 19)*

MARKS, NOS., AND KINDS OF PKGS. (15)	D/F (16)	SCHEDULE B NUMBER (17)	QUANTITY — SCHEDULE B UNIT(S) (18)	SHIPPING WEIGHT *(Pounds)* (19)

21. VALIDATED LICENSE NO./GENERAL LICENSE SYMBOL

22. ECCN *(When required)*

23. Duly authorized officer or employee

The exporter authorizes the forwarder named above to act as forwarding agent for export control and customs purposes.

24. I certify that all statements made and all information contained herein are true and correct and that I have read and understand the instructions for preparation of this document, set forth in the **"Correct Way to Fill Out the Shipper's Export Declaration."** I understand that civil and criminal penalties, including forfeiture and sale, may be imposed for making false or fraudulent statements herein, failing to provide the requested information or for violation of U.S. laws on exportation (13 U.S.C. Sec. 305; 22 U.S.C. Sec. 401; 18 U.S.C. Sec. 1001; 50 U.S.C. App. 2410).

Signature

Confidential-For use solely for official purposes authorized by the Secretary of Commerce (13 U.S.C. 301 (g)).

Title   **EXPORT CLERK**

Export shipments are subject to inspection by U.S. Customs Service and/or Office of Export Enforcement

Date

25. AUTHENTICATION *(When required)*

THESE COMMODITIES LICENSED BY U.S. FOR ULTIMATE DESTINATION — MEXICO — DIVERSION CONTRARY TO U.S. LAW PROHIBITED.

Fig. 4-13. Continued

Shipper's Name and Address		Shipper's Account Number		Not negotiable **Air Waybill** (Air Consignment note) Issued by
				Copies 1, 2 and 3 of this Air Waybill are originals and have the same validity
Consignee's Name and Address				It is agreed that the goods described herein are accepted in apparent good order and condition (except as noted) for carriage SUBJECT TO THE CONDITIONS OF CONTRACT ON THE REVERSE HEREOF. THE SHIPPER'S ATTENTION IS DRAWN TO THE NOTICE CONCERNING CARRIERS' LIMITATION OF LIABILITY. Shipper may increase such limitation of liability by declaring a higher value for carriage and paying a supplemental charge if required. To expedite movement, shipment may be diverted to motor or other carrier unless shipper gives other instructions hereon.
Issuing Carrier's Agent Name and City				Accounting Information
				SEE WARSAW NOTICE AND CONDITIONS OF CONTRACT ON REVERSE SIDE.
Agent's IATA Code		Account No.		
Airport of Departure (Addr. of first Carrier) and requested Routing				

By first Carrier	Routing and Destination			For Carrier Use only	Flight/Date	Currency	WT/VAL PPD COLL	Other PPD COLL	Declared Value for Carriage	Declared Value for Customs
Airport of Destination		Flight/Date	Flight/Date			Amount of Insurance			INSURANCE - If Carrier offers insurance, and such insurance is requested in accordance with conditions on reverse hereof, indicate amount to be insured in figures in box marked amount of insurance.	

Handling Information   These commodities licensed by the United States for ultimate destination . . . . Diversion contrary to United States law prohibited.

Fig. 4-14   A sample Air Waybill.

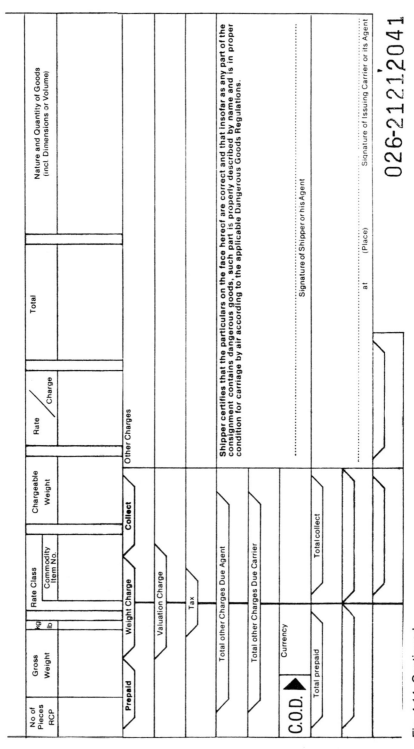

Fig. 4-14. Continued

Shipper		B/L No.
		M132–11156

Consignee

BILL OF LADING

COPY
NON - NEGOTIABLE

Notify party

ALL TERMS, CONDITIONS AND EXCEPTIONS
AS PER ORIGINAL BILL OF LADING

Pre-carriage by	Place of receipt
	KAOHSIUNG CY

"SUBJECT TO ALL THE TERMS AND
CONDITIONS OF THE APPLICABLE
TARIFF"

Ocean vessel	Voy. No.	Port of loading
AMERICA MARU	55227B	KAOHSIUNG

Port of discharge	Place of delivery	Final destination for the Merchant's reference
LOS ANGELES	TIJUANA CY	

Container No.	Seal No. Marks and Numbers	No. of Cont-	Kind of packages; description of goods ainers or pkgs.	Gross weight	Measurement
			''SHIPPER'S LOAD & COUNT''		
		3 CONTAINERS (677 CTNS)		9,014 KGS	120.32 M3
	∨∨∨∨∨∨∨∨∨∨∨∨∨∨		MODEL: H260,H670,H667		
TIJUANA B.C. MEXICO VIA LOS ANGELES CA.			MODEL: JOB NO. & CODE NO.		
MODEL: H260 C/NO. 1–235			MODEL: JOB NO. CODE NO.		
MADE IN TAIWAN REPUBLIC OF CHINA –DO–BUT H667 C/NO.1	MODEL: C/NO. 1–441 MADE IN TAIWAN REPUBLIC OF CHINA		MODEL: JOB NO. & CODE NO. ''FREIGHT COLLECT''		
	GSTU–8135538		C/S–480409 HS–41019 (192 C/T)		
	GSTU–8135939		C/S–480410 HS–41014 (192 C/T)		
	MOLU–2021646		C/S–480411 HS–41015 (293 C/T)		

*Total number of Containers or other packages or units received by the Carrier (in words)

THREE CONTAINERS ONLY

Freight and charges	Revenue tons	Rate	per	Prepaid	Collect
BOX RATE		(40'x3)	US $2,100.00/VAN (INCLUDING D.D.C.)		US$6,300.00 ∨∨∨∨∨∨∨∨∨∨∨
+ CY RECEIVING CHARGE			NT$900.00/VAN	NT$2,700.00 ∨∨∨∨∨∨∨∨∨∨	

Exchange rate (o	Prepaid at	Payable at TIJUANA	Place and date of issue TAIPEI TAIWAN JUL 30 1987
	Total prepaid in national currency	No. of original B(s)/L THREE/3	by

LADEN ON BOARD THE VESSEL

Date   JUL 30 1987   Signature

Particulars furnished by shipper

Fig. 4-15   A sample Ocean Bill of Lading.

Clean on Board. To verify shipping performance, the carrier indicates the condition of the goods upon acceptance. You should prefer to ship on a bill of lading marked "clean on board." That statement means that the carrier accepted the cargo and loaded it on board the vessel without exception.

Foul Bill. A foul bill indicates an exception—some damage is noted on the bill of lading. Discuss this with your carrier or freight forwarder to make sure you have an opportunity to exchange any damaged goods and obtain a "clean" bill.

As you have learned in the previous three chapters, most of the fundamentals of international trade are common to importing and exporting, but some major elements are specific to one or the other. The next two chapters explain those things that are unique to exporting or to importing such as: government support systems, information systems, tax considerations, tariffs, and private-sector support organizations.

5

Exporting from The United States

INTRODUCTION

SOME ASPECTS OF IMPORTING AND EXPORTING ARE NOT THE same. For example, controls are unique to exporting and the customs tariff schedule is characteristic only of importing. I have collected the specialties of exporting and importing and presented them for easy learning in chapters 5 and 6 respectively.

I have organized this chapter to explore those basics of international trade that are unique to exporting. Among other things, you will learn which public and private organizations support the export function and where to go for export information. The topics specific to export are:

- Government support
- Information sources
- Freight forwarding
- Export controls
- How to take advantage of tax incentives
- How to gain relief from unfair import practices

GOVERNMENT SUPPORT

Exporting and importing seldom are treated as equals by any country. Though governments support the import of needed raw materials, they generally place heavier emphasis on exporting, because it brings needed foreign exchange and stimulates job expansion. So it is in the United States. The United States government strongly supports exports through the International Trade Administration (ITA) of the Department of Commerce. Approximately 75% of the Department's budget is focused on this function. ITA is the major division of Commerce, and it is organized basically into external and internal arms.

The *external* arm is called the Foreign Commercial Service (FCS). Overseas, the FCS maintains offices in 120 major foreign cities in the 63 countries that are the United States' principal trading partners. More than 180 commercial offices, supported by over 500 Foreign Service Nationals, provide a full range of business, investment, and financial counseling services. These services include political and credit-risk analysis, advice on market-entry strategy, sources of financing, and major project identification, tracking, and assistance. FCS officers identify and evaluate importers, buyers, agents, distributors, and joint-venture partners for United States firms. they can introduce you to local business and government leaders and assist in trade disputes. These services are available to anyone who wants them. All you have to do is call or write your local Commerce Department District Office or the offices listed in Appendix B of this book.

The FCS Senior Commercial Officer in each country is a principal advisor to the United States Ambassador. The FCS staff gathers data on specific export opportunities, country trends affecting trade and investment, and prospects for specific industries. They also monitor and analyze local laws and practices that affect business conditions.

The domestic or *internal* arm of ITA operates 47 district offices in industrial and commercial centers throughout the United States. (See the district office addresses listed in Appendix C). These offices offer a broad range of trade-related information, as well as one-on-one counseling by experienced trade specialists. The district offices can tell exporters and other prospective businesses about:

• Trade and investment opportunities abroad

• Foreign markets for United States products and services

• Financial aid

- Insurance from the FCIA
- Tax advantages of exporting
- International trade exhibitions
- Export documentation requirements
- Economic facts on foreign countries
- Export licensing requirements

The district offices work closely with experienced regional international businesspeople through 51 District Export Councils (DECs). The 1,800 volunteer DEC members are available to:

- Counsel prospective exporters on the how-to's of international trade
- Co-sponsor seminars and workshops with the district offices
- Address business groups on international business opportunities
- Promote awareness of the trade-assistance programs of the Department of Commerce

In addition to the district offices of the ITA around the United States, the Department of Commerce also has approximately 165 desk officers at their headquarters in Washington, DC, whose job it is to be experts in assigned countries, from Afghanistan through Zimbabwe. These desk officers are resources who not only support the Secretary of Commerce and the secretary's legislative responsibilities, but also provide specific information about the laws and products of their countries to American business personnel.

Besides the district offices and the desk officers, ITA maintains an Export Counseling Center in Washington, DC, to help United States firms develop or expand markets abroad (telephone (202) 377-3181). Counselors advise exporters on the choice of Commerce Department services. United States exporters who are planning to visit Washington and would like to schedule appointments with desk officers or program specialists within the Commerce Department (and/or other agencies involved in international marketing) should contact the nearest district office or the Export Counseling Service.

EXPORT INFORMATION SOURCES

Information needed for exporting is easier to obtain than for domestic sales. Probably more information is available than one could digest in a lifetime, and the United States Department of Commerce has made it easy to acquire. For example, the Foreign Trader's Index and Trade Opportunities files are available in printed form and up-to-the-minute computer-resident data bases.

If you are planning to contact the federal government about a business matter but have no idea where to begin, the Office of Business Liaison (OBL) is a good place to start. Ask for a copy of *Business Services Directory* at the following address:

U.S. Department of Commerce
Office of Business Liaison
Room H5898C
Washington, DC 20230
202–377–3176

Government Sources

Your nearest Department of Commerce, ITA office, or the Trade Information Services Office at Commerce Department headquarters in Washington, DC offers the following information services to United States exporters.

CIMS. The Commercial Information Management System (CIMS) is the latest method developed to link you with the wealth of information that you can receive through the Department of Commerce and the worldwide offices of its United States and Foreign Commercial Service. CIMS is an electronic/computerized system that can extract from its data base market research, trade contacts, and sales leads. Your local district office can access this system, but there is a setup and per-page cost. Here are just some of the industries you can learn about:

- Analytical & Scientific Instruments
- Computers and Mini-micro Systems
- Computers and Peripheral Equipment
- Computer Software & Services
- Electronic Components
- Electronic-Component Production and Test Equipment
- Food-Processing & Packaging Equipment
- Industrial-Process Controls
- Medical Equipment

- Pollution-Control Equipment
- Telecommunications Equipment

Export Information Services for U.S. Business Firms

This booklet describes a wide range of services to assist in export activities. You can order it from the Office of Export Development, International Trade Administration, United States Department of Commerce, Washington, DC 20230. It is no charge.

The Overseas Trade Promotions Calendar

This calendar provides a schedule of United States Trade Center exhibitions and international trade fairs in which the United States plans to participate. It also includes other overseas promotional activities that the United States Department of Commerce plans and organizes. It is published regularly in the Commerce Department magazine *Business America.* You can order it from: The Office of International Marketing, International Trade Administration, United States Department of Commerce, Washington, DC.

How to Get the Most from Overseas Exhibitions

This brochure contains helpful planning tips and details the steps you must take to participate in an overseas exhibition. You can obtain a copy from the Office of Export Development, International Trade Administration, United States Department of Commerce, Washington, DC 20230. It is no charge.

Trade Opportunities Program (TOP) Notice Service

In the past, the Department of Commerce provided, for a fee, individual messages directly to subscribers, containing detailed information regarding current foreign trade leads. These leads typically included the specifications, quantities, end-use, and delivery and bid deadlines for the product or service desired by the foreign customer. "Export Opportunities", published under contract by the privately-owned daily newspaper *Journal of Commerce,* has replaced this service. The annual subscription cost is $205. "Export Opportunities" also is available on-line from the same company. Call 1-800-223-0243 for this information.

Trade Lists

A *trade list* is a list of all foreign manufacturers, wholesalers, agents, distributors, retailers, and other purchasers in a given industry, or country, included in the Commerce Department's automated Foreign Traders Index (FTI). CIMS can provide information on each firm. It includes name, address, key contact, telephone, cable, kind of business, and age of information. Trade lists are priced from $12 to $40.

Comparison Shopping Service

This service is a custom-market research report available through CIMS for your product line. It addresses overall product marketability, names of key competitors, comparison prices, customary entry, distribution, relevant trade barriers, and most other matters of interest. This service is available only for selected countries. The charge is $500 for each country surveyed.

Commercial News USA

This magazine is published ten times a year. It provides worldwide advertising for United States products and services that are available for immediate export. It is distributed to representatives, distributors, and end users. The cost for an ad in the magazine is about $250. This fee includes a listing with a photograph.

International Market Research (IMR) Surveys

These surveys provide in-depth analysis of the market. You can obtain them through CIMS for a given product category, in a given country. They are as long as 400 pages. IMRs cost $50 to $200.

Industrial Sector Analysis

This analysis provides detailed information abstracted from CIMS into convenient, 10- to 15-page reports, on a single industry in a single country. The cost of a single report is about $10.

Global Market Surveys (GMS)

This survey is a compilation of individual country market surveys (ICMS) for a given product category. Prices vary depending on the number of ICMSs within each GMS.

World Traders Data Reports (WTDRs)

This report is a background report on individual foreign firms. It contains information about each firm's business activities, its standing in the local business community, its creditworthiness, and its overall reliability and suitability as a trade contact to United States exporters. WTDRs are designed to help United States firms locate and evaluate potential foreign customers before making a business commitment. WTDRs cost $75 per report.

Ready for 1992?

During the period leading toward and after the European community completes its internal market, United States businesses need to remain aware of opportunities as well as the risks to market access. The Department of Commerce has a special office to support your interests by providing up-to-date copies of Internal Market Regulations and other information. Contact:

SINGLE INTERNAL MARKET: 1992 INFORMATION SERVICE
Office of European Community Affairs
U.S. Department of Commerce
Room 3036
14th and Constitution Ave., NW
Washington, DC 20230
or call: (202) 377-5276

Agent/Distributor Service (ADS)

ADS performs a custom overseas search for interested and qualified foreign representatives on behalf of a United States client. Foreign Commercial Service (FCS) officers abroad conduct the search and prepare a report identifying up to six foreign prospects that have personally examined the United States firm's product literature and have expressed interest in representing the firm. You can obtain ADS through CIMS. The cost is about $125 per market or specific area.

SUCCESS STORY—EXPORT INFORMATION:

A young computer whiz in his early twenties studied the trade statistics at his local ITA district office and learned that there is a need for software in Central and South America. Now his business is booming as he markets, by direct mail, to several countries in that region.

Understanding United States Foreign Trade Data

This data explains the different foreign trade classifications and valuation systems and other factors that complicate the understanding of United States foreign trade data. It is available at a cost of $7.50 from the Superintendent of Documents.

Monthly FT 410 Data

A Shipper's Export Declaration (SED) must accompany every export valued over $1000.00. This declaration is the document that you or your freight forwarder present to customs as the shipment leaves. When Customs is finished with the document, it is sent to the Department of Commerce's Bureau of Census in Anderson, Indiana, where it is entered into a computer data base. Every month, the bureau publishes a book titled *U.S. Exports, Schedule E, Commodity by Country* or the "Monthly FT 410." In minutes, you can learn a great deal from simple analysis of this data.

HOW TO USE THE FT 410
SMOKE DETECTORS—A CASE STUDY

- 43,535 smoke detectors valued at $750,000 left the United States of America during the month of June, 1984.
- 310,502 smoke detectors valued at $6,022,000 left the United States of America January thru June, 1984. Sales will be $12,000,000.
- Divide $6,022,000 by 310,502 units shipped and learn that the average declared value of each unit was $19.39.
- Most importantly, the data is shown country by country so that the user learns where the potential markets are and how many units were shipped in each case.

This data is invaluable if you are in the smoke detector business, but it also is available for an amazing list of products—everything from fruits through shoe laces, fish, golf clubs, to integrated circuits. The cost for a monthly issue of the FT410 is $9.50, and an annual subscription is $100.

Other Sources of Export Information

Besides the products offered by the Department of Commerce, several excellent books are on the market—government books and private-sector books.

U.S. Government Books. This catalog annotates almost 1,000 popular government publications organized into subject areas. You can order it at no charge from any of the 24 bookstores operated by the Government Printing Office (GPO) all around the United States. (See Appendix F for the bookstore addresses and telephone numbers.)

A Basic Guide to Exporting. The United States Department of Commerce publishes this guide. You can obtain it by writing the Superintendent of Documents, United States Government Printing Office, Washington, DC 20402, telephone number: (202) 783-3238 or by contacting any of the bookstores listed in Appendix F. The government has designed this booklet to show step-by-step how to expand an existing manufacturing business into the international marketplace. It is also an excellent resource for the small importer/exporter. The cost is about $8.00.

The EMC—Your Export Department. Describes the services provided to exporters by export-management companies as well as how to go about selecting a suitable EMC. Contact the Office of Export Development, International Trade Administration, United States Department of Commerce, Washington, D.C. 20230.

The United States Export Management Companies (EMCs) Directory. Emphasizes the marketing capability of EMC's. You can order it from: Directory of Publishers, Inc., P.O. Box 9449, Baltimore, Md. 21228.

Washington's Best Kept Secrets: A Guide to International Business. This book details all aspects of potential United States government support. You can order it from: Overseas Private Investment Corporation, 1129 20th Street, N.W., Washington, D.C. 20527. It costs about $50.00.

Exporter's Encyclopedia (Annual). This publication is a valuable resource for the serious trader's library and is chocked full of fingertip information. You can find it in most libraries or you can order it from Dun & Bradstreet International, 99 Church Street, New York, NY. Call toll free at (800) 526-0651, or if you live in NJ, call (800) 624-0324. It costs about $450.00.

An Introduction to the Overseas Private Investment Corporation (OPIC). Reviews how it can assist firms interested in investing in developing nations. You can order it from:

Overseas Private Investment Corporation, 1129 20th Street, N.W., Washington, DC 20527 at no charge.

Export-Import Bank of the United States. Explains United States export financing programs. You can order it from: Export-Import Bank of the United States, 811 Vermont Avenue, N.W., Washington, D.C. 20571 at no charge.

Carnet. Explains what a carnet is and how it can benefit exporters. It contains application forms for applying for a carnet. You can order it from: United States Council for International Business, 121 Avenue of the Americas, New York, NY 10036 at no charge.

Trade Shows and Professional Exhibits Directory. An international guide to scheduled events providing commercial display facilities, including conferences, conventions, meetings, congresses and councils, fairs and festivals, trade and industrial shows, merchandise marts, and expositions. You can find it in most libraries or you can order it from Gale Research Co., Book Tower, Detroit, MI 48226 for about $300.00.

Trade Show and Convention Guide. A guide to scheduled events including trade and industrial shows, merchandise marts, and expositions. You can find it in most libraries or you can order it from: Amusement Business, P.O. Box 24970, Nashville, TN, 37202. It costs about $100.00.

Freight Forwarder

A *freight forwarder* is a private service company licensed to support shippers and the movement of their goods. These specialists in international physical distribution act as an agent for the exporter (shipper) in moving cargo to an overseas destination. They are familiar with the following:

• The import rules and regulations of foreign countries
• The methods of shipping
• The United States government export regulations
• The documents connected with foreign trade

From the beginning, freight forwarders can assist with the order by advising on such things as freight costs, consular fees, and insurance costs. They can recommend the degree of packing, arrange for an inland carrier, find the right airline, and even arrange for the containerization of the cargo. They quote shipping rates, provide information, and book cargo space.

These firms are invaluable because they can handle everything from the factory to the final destination, including all documentation, storage, and shipping insurance, as well as routing your cargo at the lowest customs charges.

> You can become a licensed freight forwarder, but you do not have to be one to arrange movement of goods on behalf of your own shipments. Caution, don't act as a forwarder for someone else before being issued a license.

Shipper

Any person whose primary business is the sale of merchandise may, without a license, dispatch and perform freight-forwarding services on behalf of their own shipments, or on behalf of shipments or consolidated shipments of a parent, subsidiary, affiliate, or associated company. You may not, however, receive compensation from the common carrier.

A large manufacturer usually has its own shipping department which serves as its own freight forwarder, but smaller manufacturing firms and small importers/exporters seldom have the staff or the time to make their own arrangements. Often an exporter calls upon a freight forwarder to help him put together the final price quotation to a distributor. For example, when quoting C.I.F., in addition to the manufacturer's price and the commission, the forwarder can provide information on dock and cartage fees, forwarder's fees, marine insurance, ocean freight costs, duty charges, consular invoice fees, and packing charges. It's not unusual (and might be quite prudent) to review a price quotation with the freight forwarder before putting it on the telex.

Two types of freight forwarders are available: ocean and air, but most freight-forwarding businesses can do both.

An ocean freight forwarder must be licensed by the Federal Maritime Commission (FMC). The criteria to become eligible for a freight-forwarding license are:

- Three years experience in ocean freight-forwarding duties
- Necessary character to render forwarding services
- Possession of a valid surety bond

For more information on how to submit an application, contact the Office of Freight Forwarders, Bureau of Tariffs, Federal Maritime Commission, Washington, DC 20573.

Air cargo agents are administered by the International Air Transportation Association (IATA), headquartered in Montreal, Quebec, Canada. This organization, through its subsidiary, Cargo Network Services, Inc., administers the qualifications and certification of agents in the United States. You can obtain additional information by writing CNS, 300 Garden City Plaza, Suite 400, Garden City, NY 11530.

EXPORT CONTROLS

Another area in which exporting differs from importing is the licensing required to control exports. The history of export controls in the United States is based on the presumption that all exported goods and technical documentation are subject to regulation by the government. This presumption is fundamentally different than most nations, which often presume the freedom to export unless there is an explicit statement of a need to control. Therefore, the public regulation of international sales in America is often more onerous than elsewhere.

The exercise of controls by the United States varies from nonexistent (as is the case with Canada) to total embargoes (as are the cases of North Korea, Cuba, and Vietnam). Several departments have legal authority to control exports. The Department of State licenses arms, ammunition, implements of war, technical data relating thereto, and certain classified information. The Department of Justice licenses narcotics and dangerous drugs. The Nuclear Regulatory Commission licenses nuclear materials. Other exceptions exist but, in general, the Department of Commerce's control system affects most exporters. The current law (Export Administration Act of 1979), as amended, is designed to promote the foreign policy of the United States, protect the national security, and protect the domestic economy from the excessive drain of scarce materials.

The law provides for you to use three basic types of export licenses. They are as follows:

1. **General License** authorizes export without application by the exporter. It usually applies to low-dollar and low-technology items. It does not require preapproval. All you need to do is place the symbol for General License on the documentation.
2. **Qualified General License** authorizes multiple exports to a specified purchaser. It is issued pursuant to an application by the exporter.
3. **Validated License** authorizes a specific export to a

specified country and purchaser. It is issued pursuant to an application by the exporter. Several types of validated export licenses exist: individual, project, periodic, distribution, time limit, and technical data. Each license is good for one total transaction and, in general, you have two years to complete the shipment.

Export controls are organized on the Commodity Control List (CCL) according to country or by item. Some, however, focus more generally, such as those that advance the human rights cause, or those prohibiting doing business with those who boycott for ethnic or political reasons.

With few exceptions, an exporter must complete a Shipper's Export Declaration (SED) (Commerce Form 7525-V) and deposit it with the exporting carrier regardless of whether a shipment is exported under a validated or a general license.

The vast majority of all exports do not require a validated export license and require only the appropriate general license notation on the SED. Once you determine that you require a validated license for a specific export, you should submit an application for a license to the Office of Export Administration (OEA), P.O. Box 273, Washington, D.C. 20044. An application consists of a completed Form ITA-622P, "Application for Export License," and the required supporting information. Figure 5-1 is the application form for an export license.

Within 10 days after the date OEA receives the application, the office will issue the license, deny it, send the application to the next step in the licensing process, or, if you have completed the application improperly or they need additional information, return the application without action. Once you receive the approved license, you should keep the validated license on file. All you submit is the SED; however, all information on the SED must conform with that found in the validated license.

To avoid export control violations and shipping delays, you should contact your local ITA District Office or the Exporter's Service Staff, Office of Export Administration, International Trade Administration for assistance.

Form ITA-622P (REV. 4-83)
Form Approved: OMB No 0625-0001

U.S. DEPARTMENT OF COMMERCE
INTERNATIONAL TRADE ADMINISTRATION

APPLICATION FOR
EXPORT LICENSE

DATE RECEIVED *(Leave Blank)*

APPLICATION/CASE NO. *(Leave Blank)*

Information furnished herewith is subject to the provisions of Section 12 (c) of the Export Administration Act of 1979, 50 U.S.C. app. 2411 (c), and its unauthorized disclosure is prohibited by law.

1. DATE OF APPLICATION

2. APPLICANT'S REFERENCE NUMBER

3. APPLICANT'S TELEPHONE NO.

4. SPECIAL PURPOSE

5. APPLICANT

EXPORTER S I D. NO.

ADDRESS

CITY, STATE, ZIP CODE

6. PURCHASER IN FOREIGN COUNTRY
(If same as ultimate consignee, state "SAME AS ITEM 7." If same as intermediate consignee, state "SAME AS ITEM 8.")

OEA USE ONLY

NAME

ADDRESS

CITY AND COUNTRY

7. CONSIGNEE IN COUNTRY OF ULTIMATE DESTINATION

NAME

OEA USE ONLY

ADDRESS

CITY AND COUNTRY

8. INTERMEDIATE CONSIGNEE IN FOREIGN COUNTRY
(If none, state "NONE"; if unknown, state "UNKNOWN.")

OEA USE ONLY

NAME

ADDRESS

CITY AND COUNTRY

9(a) QUANTITY

(b) DESCRIPTION OF COMMODITY OR TECHNICAL DATA *(When appropriate, use Commodity Control List descriptions and include characteristics such as basic ingredients, composition, type, size, guage, grade, horsepower, model number, etc.)(Attach separate sheet if more space is needed.)*

(c) EXPORT CONTROL COMMODITY NUMBER AND PROCESSING CODE

(d) NET VALUE U.S. DOLLARS

UNIT PRICE

TOTAL PRICE

TOTAL $

10. FILL IN IF PERSON OTHER THAN APPLICANT IS AUTHORIZED TO RECEIVE LICENSE.

NAME

ADDRESS

CITY, STATE, ZIP CODE

11. IF APPLICANT IS NOT THE PRODUCER OF COMMODITY TO BE EXPORTED, GIVE NAME AND ADDRESS OF SUPPLIER. *(If unknown, state "UNKNOWN.")*

12. SPECIFIC END-USE OF COMMODITIES OR TECHNICAL DATA BY CONSIGNEE IN ITEM 7 ABOVE. IF KNOWN, GIVE NAME AND ADDRES OF END-USER IF DIFFERENT FROM ITEM 7.

13. IF APPLICANT IS NOT EXPORTING FOR HIS OWN ACCOUNT, GIVE NAME AND ADDRESS OF FOREIGN PRINCIPAL AND EXPLAIN FULLY.

14. FOREIGN AVAILABILITY (Completion Optional) This(These) ☐ commodity(ies) or similar commodities ☐ technical data ☐ is ☐ is not available outside the U.S. If available, give names and addresses of foreign producers and distributors and appropriate descriptive technical information on a separate attachment to this application. ☐ Foreign availability not known.

15. ADDITIONAL INFORMATION *(Attach separate sheet if more space is needed.)*

Fig. 5-1   A copy of an Export License Application Form.

16. APPLICANT'S CERTIFICATION: I hereby make application for a license to export, and I certify that (a) to the best of my knowledge, information and belief all statements in this application, including the description of the commodities or technical data and their end-uses, and any documents submitted in support of this application are correct and complete and that they fully and accurately disclose all the terms of the export transaction; (b) this application conforms to the instructions accompanying this application and the Export Administration Regulations; (c) I obtained the order from the order party who has completed item 17, or I negotiated with and secured the export order directly from the purchaser or ultimate consignee, or through his or their agent(s); (d) I will retain records pertaining to this transaction and make them available as required by §387.13 of the Export Administration Regulations; (e) I will report promptly to the U.S. Department of Commerce any material changes in the terms of the order or other facts or intentions of the export transaction as reflected in this application and supporting documents, whether the application is still under consideration or a license has been granted; and (f) if the license is granted, I will be strictly accountable for its use in accordance with the Export Administration Regulations and all the terms and conditions of the license.

Type
or
Print _____
(APPLICANT) (Same as Item 5.)

SIGN
HERE
IN INK _____
(SIGNATURE of person authorized to execute this application.)

Type
or
Print _____
(NAME and TITLE of person whose signature appears on the line to the left.)

17. ORDER PARTY'S CERTIFICATION (See § 372.6(b) of the *Export Administration Regulations*.)— The undersigned order party certifies to the truth and correctness of item 16(a) above, and that he has no information concerning the export transaction that is undisclosed or inconsistent with representations made to the Department of Commerce and agrees to comply with Items 16(d) and 16(e) above.

Type
or
Print _____
(Order Party)

SIGN
HERE
IN INK _____
(SIGNATURE of person authorized to sign for the Order Party.)

Type
or
Print _____
(Name and title of person whose signature appears on the line to the left.)

This license application and any license issued pursuant thereto are expressly subject to all rules and regulations of the Department of Commerce. Making any false statement or concealing any material fact in connection with this application or altering in any way the validated license issued, is punishable by imprisonment or fine, or both, and by denial of export privileges under the Export Administration Act of 1979, and any other applicable Federal statues. No export license will be issued unless this form is completed and submitted in accordance with Export Administration Regulation 372.4 (50 U.S.C. app. Sec. 2403; 15 CFR Sec. 372.4)

FOR DEPARTMENT OF COMMERCE USE ONLY

ACTION TAKEN	VALIDITY PERIOD	AUTHORITY	RATING		DV	TECH DATA
☐ APPROVED						
☐ REJECTED	MONTHS		END-USE CHECK	REEXPORT	SUPPORT DOCUMENT	TYPE OF LICENSE
DOCUMENTATION		POLICY				

_____ (Licensing officer)   _____ (No.)   _____ (Date)

_____ (Review officer)   _____   _____ (Date)

ORIGINAL
OEA FILE COPY

NOTE: Submit the first five copies of this application, Form ITA-622P (with top stub attached), to the Office of Export Administration, P.O. Box 273, Washington, D.C. 20044, retaining the sextuplicate copy of the form for your files. Remove the long carbon sheet from in front of the sextuplicate copy. Do *not* remove any other carbon sheets. Reproduction of this form is permissible, providing that content, format, size, and color of paper and ink are the same.

Fig. 5-1   (Cont.)

Hot Tips to Avoid Export Control Violations

- Determine whether you must have a validated export license. When in doubt, contact the Exporter's Services Staff, Office of Export Administration for assistance (202-377-4811).

- Fully describe commodities or technical data on export shipping documents.

- Use the applicable destination-control statement on commercial invoices, air waybills, and bills of lading, as required by Section 386.6 of the Export Administration Regulations.

- Avoid overshipments by maintaining an accurate account of the quantity and value of goods shipped against a validated export license.

- Be mindful of the expiration date on validated export licenses to avoid shipments after the applicable license has expired.

- Enter the applicable validated export license number or general license symbol on the Shipper's Export Declaration (SED).

- Make certain that shipping documents clearly identify the exporter, intermediate consignee, and ultimate consignee.

- Mail completed form ITA-622P by private courier express to: Office of Export Administration, Room 1099, United States Department of Commerce, 14th & Pennsylvania Avenue, N.W. Washington, D.C. 20230.

- Attach self-addressed, stamped postcard to front of ITA 622P stating: "This number is United States Department of Commerce case number of export license application (applicant's reference number). This number is not a license number nor is it authorization to export."

    Mail this case number back to applicant (with case number assigned) within 10 days of receipt of ITA 622P in Washington, D.C.

- Attach a private courier envelope/bill for the return of your ITA-622P.

- Important numbers:
    Status of License Application . . . .(202) 377-2752
    Export Policy & Regulations
    Clarifications.   . . . .(202) 377-4811
    Emergency License Inquiries . . . .(202) 377-2793
    Office of Export Enforcement . . . .(800) 621-2990

TAX INCENTIVES FOR EXPORTING

A prominent tax attorney once said, "Business in America? It's all about taxes." International business is no exception.

Taxes on income derived from international trade are in accordance with current laws for other income except that tax incentives for exporting are substantial. No tax incentives apply on imports.

Tax incentives for exporters amounts to approximately a 15% exclusion of the combined taxable income earned on international sales. The tax law provides for a system of tax deferrals for Domestic International Sales Corporations (DISCs) and Foreign Sales Corporations (FSCs).

Prior to December 31, 1984, the DISC was the only medium for distributing export earnings. DISCs don't require a foreign presence, and, in fact, are legal entities established only on paper. The Revenue Act of 1971 created the DISC incentive and provides for deferral of federal income tax on 50% of the export earnings allocated to the DISC, with the balance treated as dividends to the parent company. Since its enactment, the DISC has been the subject of an ongoing dispute between the United States and certain other signatories of the General Agreement on Tariffs and Trade (GATT). Other nations contended that the DISC amounted to an illegal export subsidy because it allowed indefinite deferral of direct taxes on income from exports earned in the United States.

Under new rules put into effect on the 1st of January, 1985, to receive a tax benefit that is designed to equal the tax deferral provided by the DISC, exporters must establish an office abroad. The FSC also must be a foreign corporation, maintain a summary of its permanent books of account at the foreign office, and have at least one director resident outside of the United States. Meeting the requirement of the new regulations isn't difficult for big United States-based multinationals with overseas offices and ample resources, but thousands of small businesses involved in international commerce are concerned about administrative costs and other overhead. Actually, small exporters have several options for their foreign sales operations. They may continue to export through a DISC, paying an interest charge on the deferred income, or they may join together with other exporters to own an FSC. Another alternative is that they may individually take advantage of relaxed, small FSC rules, under which they need not meet all of the tests required of large FSCs. A small FSC, one with up to $5 million of gross receipts during the taxable year, is excused from the

foreign management and foreign economic process requirements.

The mechanics of setting up a DISC or FSC are somewhat
complex, but within the capability of most accountants. Some
23 foreign countries, those that have an agreement to exchange
tax information with the United States and United States
possessions, like the Virgin Islands, Guam, and Saipan, have
established offices that are capable of providing direct assistance in setting up an FSC.

EXPORT TRADING COMPANY ACT The law passed this act on
October 8, 1982, designing it to encourage the formation of Export
Trading Companies. It establishes an Office of Export Trading
Company Affairs at the Department of Commerce, permits
banker's banks and holding companies to invest in ETCs, reduces
the restrictions on export financing provided by financial institutions, and modifies the application of the antitrust laws to certain
export trade.

Exporters with up to $10 million of annual exports may
continue to operate through DISCs, generally under the present
rules. But they must pay an annual interest charge on the
amount of tax that would be due if the post-1984 accumulated
DISC income were included in the shareholder's income. This
interest is imposed on the shareholders and paid to the Treasury of the United States.

Multiple exporters, up to 25, may jointly own an FSC and,
through the use of several classes of common stock, divide the
profits of an FSC among the several shareholders.

SUCCESS STORY—TAX ADVANTAGE. A construction engineering company formed an Export Trading Company (ETC) and
exported the services of many other smaller construction service
companies (architects, engineers, etc.) to Asia. To take advantage
of the tax exclusion and deferral opportunities on their increased
profits, they set up an FSC on the island of Saipan in the Western
Pacific.

How to Gain Relief from Unfair Import Practices

Remaining competitive in world markets is an internal management problem. The underlying elements are quantity, quality, and price. Nevertheless, government intervention is sometimes necessary when you learn about foreign firms who are not competing on what has become known as a "level playing ground."

Copies of the United States International Trade Commission's (ITC) Rules of Practice and Procedure, which set forth the procedures for the filing and conduct of investigations, are available from the Secretary, United States International Trade Commission, 701 E. Street NW., Washington, DC 20436 (telephone 202-252-1000).

The ITC Representative can investigate the following allegations:

- Countervailing duties imposed by a foreign country
- Antidumping
- General investigations of trade and tariff matters
- Investigations of costs of production
- Alleged unfair practices in import trade
- Investigations of injury from increased imports
- Worker's adjustment assistance
- Firm's adjustment assistance
- Enforcement of United States rights under trade agreements and response to certain foreign trade practices
- United States response to foreign trade practices which restrict or discriminate against United States commerce
- Investigations of market disruptions by imports from communist countries

Points of contact for instituting investigations are:

1. OFFICE OF INVESTIGATIONS
   Office of the Assistant Secretary for Trade Administration
   U.S. Department of Commerce
   Washington, DC 20230
   202-377-5497

2. TRADE REMEDY ASSISTANCE OFFICE
   U.S. International Trade Commission
   500 E Street, SW
   Washington, DC 20436
   202-252-2200 or
   1-800-343-9822

3. OFFICE OF TRADE ADJUSTMENT ASSISTANCE
   U.S. Department of Labor
   Washington, DC 20213
   202-376-2646

4. CHAIRMAN, SECTION 301 COMMITTEE
   Office of the United States Trade Representative
   600 17th Street NW
   Washington, DC
   202-395-3432

The next chapter explains those things that are unique to importing, such as tariffs, duties, and quotas.

6
How to Import into The United States

INTRODUCTION

Some aspects of importing don't apply to exporting. For example, the tariff schedule applies only to importing. I have gathered the basics unique to importing in this chapter for easy learning:

- Government support
- Information sources
- Customshouse brokers
- Getting through the customs maze
- How to use the tariff schedule
- Import quotas
- Import regulations

GOVERNMENT SUPPORT

Although you cannot think of the Customs Service of the Department of Treasury as the supporting government organization for importing in the way that the Department of Commerce is for exports, it is, nevertheless, responsible for enforcement of the relevant trade.

The Bureau of Customs is one of the nation's oldest public institutions. Provision for the service was probably the second thing the First Congress did after forming the new nation. Created in 1789 by the First Congress, it provided most of the federal government's revenue for almost 130 years. After the income tax became the nation's primary revenue source, the major responsibility of the Customs Service shifted to the administration of the Tariff Act of 1930, as amended. These duties include: (a) enforcing laws against smuggling, and (b) collecting all duties, taxes, and fees due on the volumes of goods moved through America's more than 300 ports of entry. A Customs Court, consisting of nine judges appointed by the United States President, reviews and settles disputes between importers and exporters and those that collect duties for the Bureau of Customs.

Like the Department of Commerce, the United States Customs Service is organized with an external, as well as an internal, arm.

The internal arm is organized into seven customs regions and approximately 45 district offices (see Appendices D and E for a listing of these offices).

Although not as extensive as Commerce's Foreign Commercial Service (FCS), Customs Attache's (Custom's external arm) are attached to the embassies or missions in the 12 countries listed below:

Belgium	Hong Kong	Mexico
Canada	Italy	Pakistan
England	Japan	Thailand
France	Korea	West Germany

IMPORT INFORMATION SOURCES

The Customs Service does provide considerable information related to the importing function in the form of booklets, newsletters, and seminars, that are available through the district offices or the Government Printing Office. Most of this information amounts to extractions and simplification of customs regulations. You must obtain information about how to make contacts and/or perform the import function through private-sector publishers and organizations such as Chambers of Commerce or trade associations. The following sources are helpful for learning more about importing:

Importing into the United States. This excellent booklet published by the Treasury Department through the Government Printing Office (GPO), outlines the requirements that the importer must meet to enter goods. The cost is less than $8. (See appendix F for the GPO bookstore address and telephone number in your area).

Encyclopedia of Associations. You can find this publication, which costs approximately $230, at most libraries. It provides a complete list of American and international manufacturers' associations. Order it from Gale Research Company, Brook Tower, Detroit, Mich. 48226 on their toll free number: 1-800-223-GALE.

Trade Shows and Professional Exhibits Directory. This directory is an international guide to scheduled events providing commercial display facilities, including conferences, conventions, meetings, congresses and councils, fairs and festivals, trade and industrial shows, merchandise marts, and expositions. You can find it in most libraries. Order from Gale Research Co., Book Tower, Detroit, MI 48226. It costs about $300.00.

Trade Show and Convention Guide. This booklet is a guide to scheduled events including trade and industrial shows, merchandise marts, and expositions. You can find it in most libraries. Order from: Amusement Business, P.O. Box 24970, Nashville, TN 37202. It costs about $100.

Directory of the United States Importers (Edition). This directory serves as a guide to the people, products, and marketing opportunities in the United States import industry. It costs about $250 and you can order it from The Journal of Commerce, 445 Marshall Street, Phillipsburg, NJ 08865.

Thomas Register of American Manufacturers. This resource is a compilation of manufacturers in the United States and where they are located. You might use it as a source for marketing in the United States. It is published through the Thomas Publishing Company, 1 Penn Plaza, New York, NY 10001. It is found easily in most libraries.

Directory of Manufacturers Agents. You can use this excellent publication to make contact with industrial distributors. It is published by McGraw-Hill.

Market Guide of Mass Merchandisers. Dun and Bradstreet publishes this list of contacts for salesmen.

Manufacturer's Agents Annual Directory. This up-to-date listing of United States agents is available through the AGENT AND REPRESENTATIVE, 626 North Garfield Ave., Alhambra, CA 91802.

Major Mass-Market Merchandisers. This source is published by the The Salesman's Guide, Inc. 1182 Broadway, New York, NY 10001.

Contacts Influential. This book identifies businesses, what they do, and the decisionmakers in those businesses. You can lease it from CONTACTS INFLUENTIAL, 12395 West 53rd Ave. #G-7, Arvada, CO 80002. Tel: (303) 420-1212.

CUSTOMHOUSE BROKERS

The customs broker, the custom service's liaison person with the importing public, will be needed as long as there are legal requirements and regulations pertaining to the movement of merchandise into the United States.

Like the freight forwarder for exporting, the customhouse broker is a private service company, licensed to assist importers in the movement of their goods.

Formal entries of foreign-made goods representing many billions in duty collections are filed each year with the United States customs service. Customs brokers prepare virtually all of them on behalf of importers. Some brokers are sole proprietors with a single office at one port of entry, while others are large corporations with branches in many ports throughout the country, but all are licensed and regulated by the Treasury Department.

The importer employs the customs broker as their agent and, frequently, he is their only point of contact with the United States Customs Service.

It is not necessary to employ a customhouse broker to enter goods for your own behalf; however, a bond is required if you don't. Most experienced importers will recommend the services of a broker because of the extras; that is, the comfort that a professional is supporting your project. Another good reason to procure the services of a broker is that, at some point, your time will become more valuable to you in marketing your product(s) than it might be in handling the paperwork of an entry.

A broker advises on the technical requirements of importing, preparing, and filing entry documents, obtaining the necessary bonds, depositing United States import duties, securing release of the product(s), and arranging delivery to the importer's premises or warehouse. The broker often consults with customs to determine the proper rate of duty or bases of appraisement and, on many occasions, if he is dissatisfied with the rate or value, he will pursue appropriate administrative remedies on behalf of the importer.

You can become a customs broker by (a) studying the Customs Service Regulations and learning the application of the tariff schedules, then (b) passing an examination given several times a year. This license is not necessary to act in your own behalf, but you do need it if you act as an agent for others. The cost to take the examination is approximately $300.00. You can obtain details about the examination from any Customs Service Office. Figure 6-1 shows the application form required to gain a license.

Consult the yellow pages of the local phone book for a listing of customhouse brokers in your area.

GETTING THROUGH THE CUSTOMS MAZE

A *tariff* is a schedule of duties. It is also the duty or tax imposed by a country and the duty or tax within the tariff schedule. As a tax, it is placed on goods as they cross the border between two countries.

At one time, tariffs were the primary means for the United States to raise money to support the federal government. However, in the early 1900s, when the income tax was introduced, tariffs to raise revenue became less important. Since then, tariffs have been used dominantly to protect home industries.

HISTORY NOTE The word tariff presumably comes from the Arabic term for inventory, which is ta'rif. The French word, tarif, as well as the Spanish word, tarifa, means price list or rate book. An alternate version has it that the word originated sometime after 700 A.D. At that time, near Gibraltar, there was a village called Tarifa, where a small band of thieves lived. They stopped every merchant ship and forced the captain to pay a handsome sum of money before the vessel could proceed through the Strait. Seamen began calling the money they were forced to pay, a tariff.

Bonds can be for a single entry or for a continuous term. Based on the value of the shipment, customs determines the value of the required bond. Often they require a bond three times the value of the shipment. A surety company usually requires 100% collateral in the form of an irrevocable L/C, trust

Form Approved: O.M.B. No. 1515-0076

DEPARTMENT OF THE TREASURY
UNITED STATES CUSTOMS SERVICE

APPLICATION
FOR
CUSTOMHOUSE BROKER'S LICENSE
19 U.S.C. 1641; 111.12 C.R.

Privacy Act
Statement
on Reverse
of Form

1. APPLICANT'S NAME AND ADDRESS *(Principal Office OR Home Address)*

INSTRUCTIONS: Applicants must be United States citizens. Submit application in duplicate to the District Director of the District named in Block 3. All additional continuation sheets, if required, and attachments should also be in duplicate.

2. TYPE OF LICENSE APPLIED FOR	3. CUSTOMS DISTRICT FOR WHICH LICENSE IS APPLIED
☐ Individual ☐ Corporation ☐ Partnership ☐ Association	

4. HAVE YOU EVER APPLIED FOR A CUSTOMHOUSE BROKER'S LICENSE? ☐ NO ☐ YES *(Explain in item 17)*

5. HAS THE APPLICANT *(OR ANY OFFICER OR MEMBER THEREOF)* EVER HAD A LICENSE SUSPENDED, REFUSED, REVOKED, OR CANCELED? ☐ NO ☐ YES *(Explain in item 17)*

6. IF APPLICANT HAS A CURRENT LICENSE, STATE WHEN AND FOR WHAT DISTRICT ISSUED.

7. IS THE APPLICANT *(OR ANY OFFICER OR MEMBER THEREOF)* AN OFFICER OR EMPLOYEE OF THE UNITED STATES? ☐ NO ☐ YES *(Explain in item 17)*

SECTION I — INDIVIDUALS ONLY

8. DATE OF BIRTH	9. BIRTHPLACE *(City & State)*	10. SOCIAL SECURITY NO.	11. HOME PHONE NO.	12. BUSINESS PHONE NO.

13. U.S. CITIZENSHIP ☐ NATURAL-BORN ☐ NATURALIZED-*Give Date & Place*➤

14. HAVE YOU EVER BEEN A DEFENDANT IN A CRIMINAL PROSECUTION? *(You may exclude minor traffic violations where the fine was $50 or less.)* ☐ NO ☐ YES *(Explain in item 17)*

15. DO YOU PROPOSE TO ENGAGE IN THE BUSINESS OF A CUSTOMHOUSE BROKER:

(More than one may apply. Explain answer(s) in Item 17.)

(a) ☐ ON YOUR OWN INDIVIDUAL ACCOUNT? *(State name in which business is to be conducted; if trade name, state authority for use of the name and attach evidence of such authority.)*

(b) ☐ AS A MEMBER OF A PARTNERSHIP? *(State name of partnership and list names of all the partners.)*

(c) ☐ AS AN OFFICER OF AN ASSOCIATION? *(State name of the association, the title of the office you hold, and the general nature of your duties.)*

(d) ☐ AS AN OFFICER OF A CORPORATION? *(State name of the corporation, the title of the office you hold, and the general nature of your duties.)*

(e) ☐ AS AN EMPLOYEE? *(State name and address of your employer (if different than item 1) and the nature of your employment.)*

16. LIST THE NAMES AND ADDRESSES OF SIX REFERENCES.

SECTION III — CERTIFICATION *(ALL APPLICANTS)*

INDIVIDUAL	ASSOCIATION, CORPORATION, OR PARTNERSHIP
I, _____ certify that the statements contained in the foregoing application and supporting attachments thereto are true and correct to the best of my knowledge and belief. Written notice of any change in my mailing address, any business connection, or the name and style under which I conduct my business will be given to the Commissioner of Customs.	I, _____, certify that I am an officer or partner of the applicant; that I am a licensed customhouse broker; and that the statements contained in the foregoing application and supporting attachments thereto are true and correct to the best of my knowledge and belief. The officers or partners who are licensed customhouse brokers are aware of the requirements for the exercise by them of responsible supervision and control of the transaction of the customs business of the applicant. Written notice of any change in the applicant's mailing address, name, licensed officers or partners, or the charter, certificate, articles, or other instrument of organization of the applicant will be given to the Commissioner of Customs.

23. SIGNATURE	24. DATE

Customs Form 3124 (03-03-81)

Fig. 6-1   A copy of an application for Customhouse Broker's License.

deed, or cashiers check. Bond premiums are about 2% of the value, with a minimum of about $100. The premium for a term bond is usually higher (5%). Collateral depends on the financial condition of the importer.

The Entry Process

When a shipment of goods intended for commercial use reaches the United States, it may not be entered legally until after: (a) it enters the port of entry, (b) the exporter pays the estimated duties and (c) customs authorizes delivery of the merchandise.

The process, in its simplest form, has five essential steps.

Step One: Entry. Within five working days of arrival of a shipment at a United States port of entry, entry documents must be filed. These documents consist of:

• Entry Manifest, Customs Form 7533; or Application and Special Permit for Immediate Delivery, Customs Form 3461

• Evidence of right to make entry

• Commercial invoice or a pro forma invoice

• Packing list(s) if appropriate

• Other documents necessary to determine merchandise admissibility

Form 3461 is a Special Permit for Immediate Delivery and is an alternative procedure that provides for the immediate release of a shipment. Figure 6-2 shows the form used for land shipments, and Figure 6-3 shows the form used for ocean and air shipments. You or your broker should file the application before the arrival of the goods, and, if approved, the goods won't have to sit on the dock or in a warehouse. They are released on arrival. You are allowed 10 working days to file a proper-entry summary (form 7501) and deposit estimated duties. Release under this provision is limited to the following:

• Merchandise arriving from Canada or Mexico

• Fresh fruits and vegetables for human consumption arriving from Canada or Mexico

• Articles for a trade fair

• Tariff-rate quota merchandise and, under certain circumstances, merchandise subject to an absolute quota

• Merchandise specifically authorized by customs because of perishability or inconvenience to the importer, carrier, or agent

Step Two: Examination. A Customs Officer's determination of the value of the goods and their suitability for entering has five substeps:

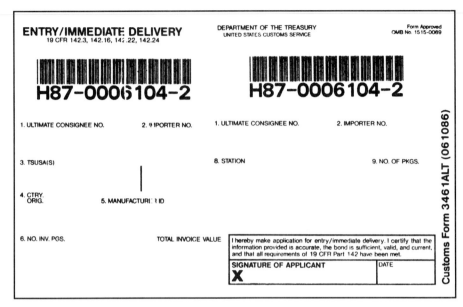

Fig. 6-2   A special immediate land entry permit.

- Valuation of the goods for customs purposes and their dutiable status
- Checking the proper markings of the goods with the country of origin
- Determining whether the shipment contains prohibited items
- Determining whether the goods are invoiced correctly
- Inventory to determine whether there are excesses or shortages of the invoiced quantities

Step Three: Valuation. This step is actually another substep of the examination process, but I offer it here as a separate step because of its importance. *Valuation* determines the value of the goods for purposes of applying any tariffs or duties.

Generally, the customs value will be the *transaction value,* or the price actually paid or payable for the merchandise when sold for exportation to the United States, plus amounts for the following items if not included in the price:

- The packing costs incurred by the buyer
- Any selling commission paid by the buyer
- The value of any assist (Note: An example of an assist would be tools, dies, molds, engineering, artwork, etc.)

Form Approved
OMB No. 1515-0069

DEPARTMENT OF THE TREASURY
UNITED STATES CUSTOMS SERVICE

ENTRY/IMMEDIATE DELIVERY

19 CFR 142.3, 142.16, 142.22, 142.24

1. ARRIVAL DATE	2. ELECTED ENTRY DATE	3. ENTRY TYPE CODE/NAME	4. ENTRY NUMBER
5. PORT	6. SINGLE TRANS. BOND	7. BROKER/IMPORTER FILE NUMBER	
	8. CONSIGNEE NUMBER		9. IMPORTER NUMBER
10. ULTIMATE CONSIGNEE NAME		11. IMPORTER OF RECORD NAME	
12. CARRIER CODE	13. VOYAGE/FLIGHT/TRIP	14. LOCATION OF GOODS—CODE(S)/NAME(S)	
15. VESSEL CODE/NAME			
16. U.S. PORT OF UNLADING	17. MANIFEST NUMBER	18. G.O. NUMBER	19. TOTAL VALUE
20. DESCRIPTION OF MERCHANDISE			
21. IT/BL/ AWB CODE	22. IT/BL/AWB NO.	23. MANIFEST QUANTITY	24. TSUSA NUMBER	25. COUNTRY OF ORIGIN	26. MANUFACTURER NO.

27. CERTIFICATION

I hereby make application for entry/immediate delivery. I certify that the above information is accurate, the bond is sufficient, valid, and current, and that all requirements of 19 CFR Part 142 have been met.

SIGNATURE OF APPLICANT

X

PHONE NO.   DATE

29. BROKER OR OTHER GOVT. AGENCY USE

28. CUSTOMS USE ONLY

☐ OTHER AGENCY ACTION REQUIRED, NAMELY:

☐ CUSTOMS EXAMINATION REQUIRED.

☐ ENTRY REJECTED, BECAUSE:

DELIVERY AUTHORIZED: SIGNATURE   DATE

Paperwork Reduction Act Notice: This information is needed to determine the admissibility of imports into the United States and to provide the necessary information for the examination of the cargo and to establish the liability for payment of duties and taxes. Your response is necessary.

Customs Form 3461 (112085)

Fig. 6-3   A special ocean and air immediate entry permit.

- Any royalty or license fee that is required from the buyer as a condition of the sale
- The proceeds from the sale of the imported goods that accrue to the seller

If you cannot use the transaction value for the goods, then you must use secondary bases in the following order of precedence:

- Transaction value of identical merchandise
- Transaction value of similar merchandise
- Deductive value
- Computed value

Step Four: Classification. This step too, is a substep of the examination process designed to determine the tariff or duty rate. Classification is initially the responsibility of the importer, customhouse broker, or other person preparing the entry papers. Familiarity with the Tariff Schedule of the United States (TSUS) and the Harmonized System (HS) Tariff Schedule of the United States facilitates the process.

Step Five: Liquidation. The classification and valuation, as well as other required import information, are reviewed for (a) correctness, (b) as a proper basis for appraisement, and (c) for agreement of the submitted data with the merchandise actually imported. If it is accepted without changes, it is liquidated "as entered." This step is finalized in the traditional way of posting a notice on the public bulletin board at the customhouse. The bulletin board is now a computer printout.

After the liquidation, an importer may pursue claims for adjustment or refund by filing, within 90 days, a protest on Custom's Form 19. Time limits do not begin to run until the date of posting. If, after further review, the importer is still not satisfied, he may file a summons with the United States Customs Court of International Trade.

HOW TO USE THE HARMONIZED TARIFF SCHEDULE

The United States recently joined the European Community, Canada, and Japan in the use of a new tariff schedule called the Harmonized System (HS). This schedule is an international, multipurpose, classification system designed to improve the collection of import and export statistics as well as for customs purposes. Intended to serve as a core for national systems, it promotes a high degree of international uniformity in the presentation of custom's tariffs and foreign trade statistics. The HS replaced the Tariff Schedule of the United States (TSUS) and the Tariff Schedule of the United States Annotated (TSUSA), as the United States' import schedule. It also replaced Schedule B as the United States export code. (see Appendix G for the procedures to use the TSUSA should you need to refer to that schedule.)

Advantages of the Harmonized System

The advantages of the Harmonized System are:

- The world will use the same system.
- Imports and exports will use this system, and you will not have to look at different numbers for different countries.
- It allows the utilization of standard documents.
- It facilitates the classification process.
- It's a progressive system.
- It provides for better trade statistics.
- It provides better export assistance.
- It protects trade concessions.
- It provides for uniform collections.
- It offers a means for uniform enforcement.

HISTORY NOTE For decades, the international trading community was confronted with problems caused by the number of differing classification systems for the movement of goods in international trade. In 1970, representatives of the Customs Cooperation Council (CCC), formerly known as the Brussels Tariff Nomenclature (BTN), undertook a study of commodity description and coding, hoping to develop a system capable of meeting the principal requirements of customs authorities, statisticians, carriers, and producers. The result of the study was that the development of such a system was not only feasible, but imperative. Some 13 years later they completed the "Harmonized Commodity Description and Coding System" and had a convention for its implementation. Forty-eight countries and more than a dozen private and public organizations participated in its development.

Description of the Harmonized System

The Harmonized System (HS) is about the size of a major city's telephone book. It is available through the Government Printing Office in three-hole, loose-leaf form for about $60. The stock number is 040-000-00516-1.

The HS is a complete product classification system, which is organized by a numbering system. To assist the user, a section in the front of the book gives instructions known as General Notes and General Rules of Interpretation (GRI). These notes and rules explain the use and interpretation of the schedule and a table of contents.

At the international level, about 5000 article descriptions are grouped into 21 sections and arranged into 97 chapters (although chapter 77 is empty). The United States version has 22 sections instead of 21, and 99 chapters. Chapter 98 includes information from the "old" TSUSA Schedule 8 related to off-shore production (articles 806.20, 806.30 and 807). Chapter 99 contains information transformed from the TSUSA Schedule 9. The 22 sections and their chapter headings are listed in a table of contents in the front of the HS.

Case Study—Guitars. Let's hypothesize that you are an importer of guitars valued at less than $100. Your order from West Germany arrives. Within 5 working days you must present the documents listed in step one of the entry process to customs.

Note: If the guitars were perishable, or you had a special scheduling problem, you could have applied in advance for their immediate delivery, using Special Entry Permit Form 3461.

In this case, let us assume there was no need for immediate entry, so we proceed as a normal, formal entry.

Let's further assume you used an L/C to make payment, so you can only pick up your entry documents after you square your account with your banker. The invoice shows 100 guitars at $89 each, for a total of $8,900. This value is the transaction value for purposes of valuation. Because the value is over $1000, you must make a formal entry. Had the value been under $1000, the informal entry process would have been much simpler; you could have done your own paperwork, and you would not need a bond. Figure 6-4 shows an Entry Summary, the basic form used for both formal and informal entry. Table 6-1 shows the difference between a formal and an informal entry.

Had the goods been for your personal use and you had been out of the country for more than 48 hours, the first $400 ($800 when returning from a United States insular possession) would have been exempt, the next $1000 dutied at 10%, and the remainder at the ad valorem rate from the tariff schedule.

Beginners sometimes ask, "What if I entered the goods for personal use in small quantities and then sold them?" One customs agent told the author, "They may get away with it the

DEPARTMENT OF THE TREASURY
UNITED STATES CUSTOMS SERVICE

ENTRY SUMMARY

(1) Entry No.	(2) Entry Type Code	3. Entry Summary Date
4. Entry Date	(5) Port Code	
6. Bond No.	7. Bond Type Code	8. Broker/Importer File No.
10. Consignee No.	(11) Importer of Record Name and Address	(12) Importer No.

9. Ultimate Consignee Name and Address

	(13) Exporting Country	14. Export Date
	(15) Country of Origin	16. Missing Documents
State		
	(17) I.T. No.	(18) I.T. Date
20. Mode of Transportation	21. Manufacturer I.D.	22. Reference No.
24. Foreign Port of Lading	25. Location of Goods/G.O. No.	
27. Import Date		

(19) B L or AWB No.

(23) Importing Carrier

26. U.S. Port of Unlading

Fig. 6-4   A sample entry summary.

| (28) Line No. | (29) Description of Merchandise | | | (33) (A) Entered Value | (34) (A) T.S.U.S.A. Rate | (35) Duty and I.R. Tax | |
| | (30) (A) T.S.U.S.A. No. (B) ADA CVD Case No. | (31) (A) Gross Weight (B) Manifest Qty. | (32) Net Quantity in T.S.U.S.A. Units | (B) CHGS (C) Relationship | (B) ADA/CVD Rate (C) I.R.C. Rate (D) Visa No. | Dollars | Cents |

↓ U.S. CUSTOMS USE ↓

TOTALS

A. Liq. Code	B. Ascertained Duty	(37) Duty
	C. Ascertained Tax	(38) Tax
	D. Ascertained Other	(39) Other
	E. Ascertained Total	(40) Total

(36) Declaration of Importer of Record (Owner or Purchaser) or Authorized Agent

I declare that I am the ☐ importer of record and that the actual owner, purchaser, or consignee for customs purposes is as shown above. OR ☐ owner or purchaser or agent thereof.

I further declare that the merchandise ☐ was obtained pursuant to a purchase or agreement to purchase and that the prices set forth in the invoice are true. OR ☐ was not obtained pursuant to a purchase or agreement to purchase and the statements in the invoice as to value or price are true to the best of my knowledge and belief.

I also declare that the statements in the documents herein filed fully disclose to the best of my knowledge and belief the true prices, values, quantities, rebates, drawbacks, fees, commissions, and royalties and are true and correct, and that all goods or services provided to the seller of the merchandise either free or at reduced cost are fully disclosed. I will immediately furnish to the appropriate customs officer any information showing a different state of facts.

(41) Signature of Declarant, Title, and Date

Notice required by Paperwork Reduction Act of 1980. This information is needed to ensure that importers/exporters are complying with U.S. Customs laws, to allow us to compute and collect the right amount of money, to enforce other agency requirements, and to collect accurate statistical information on imports. Your response is mandatory.

Customs Form 7501 (030984)

Fig. 6-4   (Cont.)

Table 6-1 Formal vs. Informal Entry

	Informal	Formal
Value	Less than $1000.00*	$1000.00 or greater
Bond	No	Yes
Duties	Pay on entry	Pay within 10 days†
Liquidation	On the spot	Liquidation notice
Forms Required	7501, invoice, B/L, check ($$$ duties), Packing list,	7501, Invoice, B/L packing list, check ($$$ duties), other agency documents, bond

*For some articles, formal entry is specified regardless of value (check your local customs service office or custom house broker).

†An example of a good that might require immediate payment would be an item under quota.

first time, but we (the computers) remember, and sooner or later, we'll catch them. The penalty is at least a $5000 fine."

Full, complete, and honest disclosure is the responsibility of the importer. The penalties are severe and not worth the gamble. Make your money and pay your duties.

In this example, because the value is $1000 or greater ($8,900), you must file a formal entry. For the formal or informal entry process, you need to classify the product. Begin by scanning the table of contents for the general category within which your product fits. In this case, "Musical instruments" is in Section XVIII, Chapter 92.

If you have a copy of the HS available, turn to page 92-2. If not, flip to Figure 6-5 of this book. Figure 6-5 is a copy of page 92-2 from the Harmonized Schedule related to our case study about guitars.

Run your finger down the page until you find "guitars: valued not over $100." In this case, the classification of guitars is straightforward, but keep in mind that classifying a product is usually the most difficult part of using any tariff schedule. The correct classification can save you money and heartache. Consult the customs service or your customhouse broker if you have any doubts.

The heading for this product is 9202.90.20. The first two digits refer to the chapter number, in this case chapter 92. The

TARIFF SCHEDULE OF THE UNITED STATES ANNOTATED

92-2   (Converted to the Harmonized System and reflecting final MTN concession rates of duty)

Heading	Stat. Suf- fix	Article Description	Units of Quantity	Rates of Duty General	Rates of Duty Special	2
9201		Pianos, including player pianos; harpsichords and other keyboard stringed instruments:				
9201.10.00	00	Upright pianos	No......	5.3%	Free (A,E)	40%
9201.20.00	00	Grand pianos	No......	5.3%	Free (A,E)	40%
9201.90.00	00	Other	No......	5.3%	Free (A,E)	40%
9202		Other string musical instruments (for example, guitars, violins, harps):				
9202.10.00	00	Played with a bow	No......	4.9%	Free (A,E)	37.5%
9202.90		Other:				
		Guitars:				
9202.90.20	00	Valued not over $100 each	No......	6.8%	Free (A,E)	40%
9202.90.40	00	Other	No......	13%	Free (A,E)	40%
92u2.90.60	00	Other	No......	7%	Free (A,E)	40%
9203.00		Keyboard pipe organs; harmoniums and similar key- board instruments with free metal reeds:				
9203.00.40	00	Keyboard pipe organs	No......	Free		35%
9203.00.80	00	Other	No......	5.3%	Free (A,E)	40%
9204		Accordions and similar instruments; mouth organs:				
9204.10		Accordions and similar instruments:				
9204.10.40	00	Piano accordions	No......	4.7%	Free (A,E)	40%
9204.10.80	00	Other	No......	5.1%	Free (A,E)	40%
9204.20.00	00	Mouth organs	Doz.....	4.7%	Free (A,E)	40%
9205		Other wind musical instruments (for example, clarinets, trumpets, bagpipes):				
9205.10.00		Brass-wind instruments	....	5.8%	Free (A,E)	40%
	40	Valued not over $10 each	No.			
	80	Valued over $10 each	No.			
9205.90		Other:				
		Woodwind instruments:				
9205.90.20	00	Bagpipes	No......	Free		40%
9205.90.40		Other	....	4.9%	Free (A,E)	40%
	20	Clarinets	No.			
	40	Saxophones	No.			
	60	Flutes and piccolos (except bamboo)	No.			
	80	Other	No.			
9205.90.60	00	Other	No......	3.4%	Free (A,E)	40%
9206.00		Percussion musical instruments (for example, drums, xylophones, cymbals, castanets, maracas):				
9206.00.20	00	Drums	X.......	4.8%	Free (A,E)	40%
9206.00.40	00	Cymbals	X.......	Free		40%
9206.00.60	00	Sets of tuned bells known as chimes, peals or carillons	X.......	2.5%	Free (A,E)	50%
9206.00.80	00	Other	X.......	5.3%	Free (A,E)	40%

Fig. 6-5   The tariff schedule of the United States Annotated.

next two refer to the heading, the next two to the international subdivision, then the United States subdivision, and finally the United States statistical subdivision.

Now, draw your finger across the page. Note that there are three vertical columns, each with an ad valorem duty rate. In Column 1 "general," the rate is 6.8%. This rate is for developed countries such as England, France, or Germany. Thus, because your guitars came from Germany, you will pay 6.8% of $8,900, or $605.20 ad valorem duty.

Note that the duty rate shown in column 1, "special," is free for country groups A and E. The countries in these groups are listed in the "special" category in the front of the book under head notes. See Figures 6-6 and 6-7 which are excerpts from the general headnotes found in the front of the tariff schedule, and which show the countries in these categories.

Group A are the Generalized Systems of Preference (GSP) countries, or those designated by the United Nations as "developing." To assist in their economic growth, they get special preference and therefore, pay no tariff. Group E is a list of Caribbean-Basin Economic-Recovery-Act countries. In this case, the United States is assisting in their economic recovery. They also get special tariff preference and pay no duties on most goods.

The third column labeled "2," shows a rate of 40% for guitars valued under $100. This column shows the ad valorem duty rate for countries under communist domination or control, such as Albania, North Korea, Soviet Union, etc. If the guitars had come from Russia, instead of Germany, the ad valorem duty paid to the United States Treasury would be 40% of $8,900 or $3560.

Having estimated your duties as $605.20, the next step is to fill out the required entry documents and post surety in the form of cash or evidence of having a bond (minimum of $10,000). If a customhouse broker makes the entry for you, the broker may use their bond. This procedure is not automatic. In many cases they will assist you to obtain your own bond. There are three types of bonds: "Term," which covers entry through only one port of entry; "General," which covers all United States ports; and "Continuous," which can substitute for both.

After filling out the commercial-custom's invoice, the special (consular) custom's invoice, the bill of lading, and the entry form, the goods may be picked up from the carrier.

Remember, you or your agent (customhouse broker) originally classified and estimated the duties owed. Final liquida-

(A) The following countries, territories, and associations of countries eligible for treatment as one country (pursuant to section 502(a)(3) of the Trade Act of 1974 (19 U.S.C. 2462(a)(3)) are designated beneficiary developing countries for the purposes of the Generalized System of Preferences, provided for in Title V of the Trade Act of 1974, as amended (19 U.S.C. 2461 et seq.):

Independent Countries

Angola	Djibouti	Madagascar	Sierra Leone
Antigua and Barbuda	Dominica	Malawi	Singapore
Argentina	Dominican Republic	Malaysia	Solomon Islands
Bahamas	Ecuador	Maldives	Somalia
Bahrain	Egypt	Mali	Sri Lanka
Bangladesh	El Salvador	Malta	Sudan
Barbados	Equatorial Guinea	Mauritania	Suriname
Belize	Federated States of	Mauritius	Swaziland
Benin	Micronesia	Mexico	Syria
Bhutan	Fiji	Morocco	Taiwan
Bolivia	Ghana	Mozambique	Tanzania
Botswana	Grenada	Nauru	Thailand
Brazil	Guatemala	Nepal	The Gambia
Brunei Darussalam	Guinea	Niger	Togo
Burkina Faso	Guinea Bissau	Oman	Tonga
Burma	Guyana	Pakistan	Trinidad and Tobago
Burundi	Haiti	Panama	Tunisia
Cameroon	Honduras	Papua New Guinea	Turkey
Cape Verde	India	Peru	Tuvalu
Central African	Indonesia	Philippines	Uganda
Republic	Israel	Republic of Marshall	Uruguay
Chad	Jamaica	Islands	Vanuatu
Chile	Jordan	Rwanda	Venezuela
Colombia	Kenya	Saint Lucia	Western Samoa
Comoros	Kiribati	Saint Vincent and	Yemen Arab Republic (Sanaa)
Congo	Korea, Republic of	the Grenadines	Yugoslavia
Costa Rica	Lebanon	Sao Tome and Principe	Zaire
Cote d'Ivoire	Lesotho	Senegal	Zambia
Cyprus	Liberia	Seychelles	Zimbabwe

Fig. 6-6   Countries that receive free tariffs.

UNITED STATES TARIFF SCHEDULE

Non-Independent Countries and Territories

Anguilla	French Polynesia	Pitcairn Islands
Aruba	Gibraltar	Saint Christopher and Nevis
Bermuda	Heard Island and	Saint Helena
British Indian Ocean	McDonald Islands	Tokelau
Territory	Hong Kong	Trust Territory of the
Cayman Islands	Macau	Pacific Islands (Palau)
Christmas Island (Australia)	Montserrat	Turks and Caicos Islands
Cocos (Keeling) Island	Netherlands Antilles	Virgin Islands, British
Cook Islands	New Caledonia	Wallis and Futuna
Falkland Islands	Niue	Western Sahara
(Islas Malvinas)	Norfolk Island	

Associations of Countries (treated as one country)

Member Countries of the Cartagena Agreement (Andean Group)	Association of South East Asian Nations (ASEAN)
Consisting of:	Consisting of:
Bolivia	Brunei
Colombia	Indonesia
Ecuador	Malaysia
Peru	Phillipines
Venezuela	Singapore
	Thailand

Member Countries of the Carribbean Common Market (CARICOM)

Consisting of:

Antigua and Barbuda	Jamaica
Bahamas	Montserrat
Barbados	Saint Christopher and Nevis
Belize	Saint Lucia
Dominica	Saint Vincent and
Grenada	the Grenadines
Guyana	Trinidad and Tobago

(B) The following beneficiary countries are designated as least-developed beneficiary developing countries pursuant to section 504(c)(6) of the Trade Act of 1974, as amended:

Bangladesh	Equatorial Guinea	Rwanda
Benin	Gambia, The	Sao Tome and Principe
Bhutan	Guinea	Sierra Leone
Botswana	Guinea-Bissau	Somalia
Burkina Faso	Haiti	Sudan
Burundi	Lesotho	Tanzania
Cape Verde	Malawi	Togo
Central African Republic	Maldives	Uganda
Chad	Mali	Western Samoa
Comoros	Nepal	Yemen Arab Republic
Djibouti	Niger	(Sanaa)

Whenever an eligible article is imported into the customs territory of the United States directly from one of the countries designated as a least-developed beneficiary developing country, it shall be entitled to receive the duty-free treatment provided for in subdivision (c)(ii)(C) of this note without regard to the limitations on preferential treatment of eligible articles in section 504(c) of the Trade Act, as amended (19 U.S.C. 2464(c)).

Fig. 6-7   Countries that receive free tariffs.

tion of this transaction by the customs service could take as much as several months but must be finalized (with exceptions) within 1 year. You will receive notice of the date of liquidation and what amounts are due, if any.

IMPORT QUOTAS

The importation of certain products—usually to protect infant industries or established industries under marketing pressure from foreign countries—are controlled by quantity. Specific legislation establishes quotas for this control, and the Commissioner of Customs has no right to change or modify the quotas. United States import quotas are divided into two types: absolute and tariff-rate.

Absolute Quotas

These quotas are *quantitative quotas,* that is, no more than the amount specified may be permitted during the quota period. Some are global, while others apply only to certain countries.

Tariff-rate Quotas

These quotas provide for the entry of a specified quantity at a reduced rate of duty during a given period. Quantities entered in excess of the quota for the period are subject to higher duty rates.

The status of quotas are maintained by a central Customs Service computer in Washington, DC. You can obtain access to current quota status by taped telephone message. These telephone numbers are available from your local custom's office.

SPECIAL IMPORT REGULATIONS

Many countries require a license to import, but the United States does not. Thousands of products are imported freely with no restrictions. Although the importation of goods does not require a license from the customs service, certain classes of merchandise might be prohibited or restricted by other agencies (a) to protect the economy and the security of the country, (b) to safeguard health, or (c) to preserve domestic plant and animal life. The importer is wise to inquire (complete with samples and specifications) with the regulatory body involved, well before entering into any business arrangements. Cases exist in which the importer ended up with a warehouse full of products unfit or prohibited from entering the United States.

Agricultural Commodities

The United States Food and Drug Administration and the Department of Agriculture control or regulate the importation of most animals, animal foods, insects, plants, and poultry products.

Arms, Ammunition, and Radioactive Materials

The Bureau of Alcohol, Tobacco, and Firearms of the Department of the Treasury, Washington, DC 20226 prohibits the importation of implements of war except when they issue a license. Even temporary importation, movement, and exportation is prohibited unless licensed by the Office of Munitions Control, Department of State, Washington, DC 20520. Of course, the Nuclear Regulatory Commission controls all forms of radioactive materials and nuclear reactors.

Consumer Products

Such consumer products as refrigerators, freezers, dishwashers, water heaters, television sets, and furnaces (and other energy-using products) are regulated by the Consumer Products Efficiency Branch of the Department of Energy.

Food, Drugs, Cosmetics, and Medical Devices

The Federal Food, Drug, and Cosmetic Act governs the importation of food, beverages, drugs, devices, and cosmetics. This act is administered by the Food and Drug Administration of the Department of Health and Human Services, Rockville, MD 20857.

Gold, Silver, Currency, and Stamps

Provisions of the National Stamping Act, enforced by the Department of Justice, Washington, DC, 20530, regulate some aspects of importing silver and gold.

Pesticides and Toxic and Hazardous Substances

Three acts control the importation of these substances: Insecticide, Fungicide, and Rodenticide Act of 1947; Toxic Substances Control Act of 1977; and the Hazardous Substances Act. You can obtain further information from the Environmental Protection Agency, Washington, DC 20460.

Textile, Wool, and Fur Products

The Textile Fiber Products Identification Act requires all textile fiber products to be stamped, tagged, and labeled according to their requirements. Similarly, the Wool Products Labeling Act of 1939 requires you to mark all wool products according to their requirements. You must label fur, not to be left out, as required by the Fur Products Labeling Act. You can obtain regulations and pamphlets containing the text of these labeling acts from the Federal Trade Commission, Washington, DC 20580.

Trademarks, Tradenames, and Copyrights

The Customs Reform and Simplification Act of 1979 strengthened the protection afforded trademark owners against the importation of articles bearing counterfeit marks. In general, articles bearing trademarks, or marks that copy or simulate a registered trademark of a United States or foreign corporation, are prohibited importation. Similarly, the Copyright Revision Act of 1976 provides that the importation into the United States of copies of a work acquired outside the United States, without authorization of the copyright owner, is an infringement of the copyright.

Wildlife and Pets

The United States Fish and Wildlife Service, Department of Interior, Washington, D.C. 20240 controls the importation of (a) wild or game animals, birds, and other wildlife, or any part or product made therefrom; and (b) the eggs of wild or game birds. The importation of birds, cats, dogs, monkeys, and turtles is subject to the requirements of the United States Public Health Service, Center for Disease Control, Quarantine Division, located in Atlanta, Georgia 30333.

The preceding five chapters have presented the basics of import and export. Now that you understand them, the next chapter shows you how to put these fundamentals into practice in your own import-export business.

7

Setting Up Your Own Import/Export Business

"I WANT TO START MY OWN IMPORT COMPANY TO BUY BEAD FRINGE from Egypt and sell it in the United States. How do I start?"

"Why bead fringe?"

Teresa Brown responded, "Because I studied costume design in college and worked in the field. I know where the best bead fringe is and I want to get into the business."

Teresa sounds ready to start her own import/export business. But she's not quite ready yet. What Ms. Brown forgot was that an import/export business is a business! It takes capital, management, goals, and, above all, planning.

By incorporating what you've learned about the fundamentals of import/export in chapters 2 through 6 with the methods explained in this chapter, you should be ready to start your own import/export business or work in the international department of an existing manufacturing firm.

The first part of this chapter describes the mechanics of start-up. The second part shows you how to develop a business plan so that you can raise capital and grow.

THE MECHANICS OF START-UP

Start-up Capital

In the initial stages of starting your own import/export business, the funds needed to support expenses most likely will come from your own pocket. It is possible to begin an import/export business with as little as $1000 a year.

When your personal financial outlook will not sustain those costs (expenses of start-up), you must look for outside financial assistance. Unfortunately, banks are seldom the source of start-up capital. Why? Banks do not take risks. They generally expect a track record and collateral. Catch 22? Where can you go for financing? Most often, the source is relatives and/or friends, people who know you and believe in you. Even they might want a description of your intended business, often in the form of a business plan. So, from the beginning, you should develop a written plan for your business. You might want to skip to the second part of this chapter immediately to learn how to write that plan. You can return to this section when you complete your business plan.

Business Name

Think of a name for your business. The company's name should reflect what your business does. For example, you easily can visualize the nature of the business of the "Southeast U.S. Furniture Import." It gives a more accurate picture of that company than would "Kim Yee and Son." Teresa Brown named her company International Costumes. In this case, because the name does not contain the owner's surname, most states would require a request to use a fictitious name, or DBA (doing business as). If the name of your business included your last name, you might not be required to file a fictitious name approval with your local county. The cost for registering your fictitious name is about $10 in most counties. There is also a requirement to publish that name in a newspaper for several days. That cost is usually not more than $20 to $30.

The Business Organization

Next, decide how you will organize your business. The three common legal forms are sole proprietorship, partnership, or corporation. Most start-up import/export businesses begin as proprietorships or partnerships. They find little need to take on the extra paperwork and reporting requirements of a corporation, in the beginning. Select the form of your business based on the intent, complexity, tax implications, and liability requirements of the business. If in doubt, consult a lawyer. Partnership agreements and incorporation papers can be expensive, requiring as little as a few hundred dollars or as much as several thousand dollars.

Business License

The United States does not require a special license for importing or exporting. That is, there is no regulatory body that requires you to show special qualifications in order to be an importer or exporter. However, like any other business, you probably must meet local and state licensing requirements. It is possible that the foreign country you are doing business with will require a license as well. Check with your freight forwarder.

Seller's Permit

Most states have a sales tax. In order to ensure collection, a board of equalization or sales tax board requires a seller's permit. Usually the state controls these permits. As you begin your own import/export business, you should investigate your local laws.

Financial Records

Open a separate bank account in the name of your business. Keep accurate records, and pass all business income and expenses through your business account. Do not pay personal expenses from this account or otherwise mix personal income or expenses with business income and expenses. You may list personal "capital contributions" and "capital withdrawals," but keep these infrequent and in reasonably large sums—don't take out money in dribbles and drops.

Accounting

From the beginning, learn to keep a simple set of books to feed into your Internal Revenue Service (IRS) Schedule C (Profit or Loss from Own Business or Profession) at tax time. Keep a careful record (all receipts) of all business expenses, and invoice all work on your letterhead paper. At a minimum, you will need a general ledger organized into four sections: expenses, income, receivables (sales invoiced), and payables (bills received). For example, you should list your expenses, like the cost of your trip to Hong Kong or Paris, chronologically, by month, down the left margin of the expense section. Across the page, the categories should correspond to the categories called for by the Schedule C. Check current IRS publications.

What kind of expenses should you expect in your own import/export business?

- Stationary and business cards
- Telephone, answering machines, adding machine, copier, typewriter, facsimile, telex machine
- Rent, utilities, office furniture
- Inventory
- Business checking account
- Salaries and other staff expenses
- Travel

Table 7-1 shows an example of the categories of expenses shown in the expense section of your general ledger. You should set up the other sections of your ledger similarly.

Table 7-1 Typical Expenses

Date	Utilities	Telephone/ Telex	Travel Air	Tavel Auto	Office Expense
January					
February					
March					

The Office

You can set up an office in your home or elsewhere. The volume and complexity of your business will determine the location and outfitting. In the beginning, you might do business by letter and only use the telex and part-time employees occasionally. However, as your import/export business grows, you might need warehouse space for inventory and a larger office for a growing staff.

Employees

As your office and trading staff grows, the complexity of paperwork and record keeping also will grow. Prior to hiring anyone, you must obtain an employers I.D. number from the IRS, and consider Worker's Compensation and Benefits insurance.

Business Insurance

Other business insurance that you should consider on a case-by-case basis are Liability, Disability, FCIA Umbrella policy, and a customs bond.

Support Team

Early in the establishment of your import/export business, you should develop a relationship with your international support team. After a brief period of shopping around, settle on a long-term relationship with (a) an international banker; (b) a freight forwarder; (c) a customhouse broker, (d) an international accountant, and (e) an international attorney. Also, consider contacting the Small Business Administration (SBA) if you run into problems. Members of the SBA's Service Corps of Retired Executives (S.C.O.R.E.) often are available to provide free advise.

The Ten Commandments
of Starting an Overseas Business

1. Limit the primary participants to people who can agree and contribute directly and who are experienced in some form of international business.
2. Define your import/export market in terms of what is to be bought, precisely by whom, and why.
3. Concentrate all available resources on two or three products or objectives within a given time period.
4. Obtain the best information through your own industry.
5. Write down your business plan and work from it.
6. "Walk on two legs." Pick a good freight forwarder or customhouse broker to walk alongside your banker.
7. Translate your literature into the language(s) of the country(s) in which you will do business.
8. Use the services of the United States Departments of Commerce and Treasury.
9. Limit the effects of your inevitable mistakes by starting slowly.
10. Communicate frequently and well with your international contacts, and visit the overseas markets and manufacturers.

THE BUSINESS PLAN

Teresa Brown had already thought through the hard international marketing questions suggested in chapter 3. She knew her product and knew where to buy it. As a result of her work experience, she also knew how to market the product in the United States. But what she hadn't done was put those thoughts on paper.

In the beginning, you might have only a notion of your plan tucked away in your head. As the business grows, it will be necessary to formalize your plan and stick to it. Putting out brushfires in order to maintain marginal survival is hardly a wise use of anyone's time.

The underlying concept of a business plan is to write out your thoughts. By raising, then systematically answering basic operational questions, you force self-criticism. Once on paper, others can read it, and you can invite their opinions. Don't let your ego get in your way. Ask for constructive criticism from the most experienced people you can find. Often it is better to ask strangers, because friends and relatives tend to want to shield you from hurt. Explain to your readers that you want to hear the bad news and the good news. The more eyes that see the plan, the more likely you will: (a) identify hazards while you still can act or avoid them, and (b) spot opportunities while you easily can act to maximize them.

A business plan can be as brief as 10 pages and as long as 50. On the average, they run about 20 pages. Every outline is usually about the same. Table 7-2 suggests an outline format for your business plan.

How To Begin the Business Plan

Stop everything, and begin writing. The first draft of your plan will contain about 80% of the finished draft and you can finish it in less than 2 days. One measure of the success of the process is the amount of pain it causes you. By looking at your business as an onlooker would, you might find that some of your vision, a pet project for instance, might have to be abandoned.

Table 7-2 Business Plan Outline

Cover Sheet: Name, principals, address, etc.

International Costumes, Inc.
Business Plan
Fiscal Year 19xx

Statement of Purpose:

Table of Contents: (corresponds to each exhibit)

A. Executive summary
B. Description of the business
C. Product-line plan
D. Sales and market plan
E. Operations plan
F. Organization plan
G. Financial plan
H. Supporting documents
I. Summary

Exhibits:

Exhibit A   Executive Summary
1. Written last, summarizes in global terms the entire plan; succinct expression of long- and short-term goals

Exhibit B   Description of the Business
1. Goals: Long and short term.
   Financial
   Nonfinancial
2. Strategies
   Product line
   Sales and marketing
   Product development
   Operations
   Organizational
   Financial
3. Location
   Reasons

Exhibit C   Product-line Plan
1. Product line and products
   Description
   Price
   Costs
   Historical volume
   Future expectations

Table 7-2 (Cont.)

2. Competition's product line and product position
    Pricing
    Advertising and promotion

Exhibit D   Sales and Market Plan
1. Person(s) responsible for generating product line and product sales
2. Competition's approach to sales and marketing

Exhibit E   Operations Plan
1. Production and operations function
    Production scheduling
    Inventory (product line and product)
2. Capital expenditures (if required)

Exhibit F   Organization Plan
1. Organization's structure
    Organization chart
    Resumes of key personnel
    Managerial style

Exhibit G   Financial Plan
1. Summary of operating and financial schedules
2. Schedules (refer to Figures 7-1, 7-2, 7-3 and 7-4)
    Capital equipment
    Balance sheet
    Cash flow (break-even analysis)
    Income projections
    Pro forma cash flow
    Historical financial reports for existing business
    (Balance sheets for past three years: Income statements for past three years; Tax returns)

Exhibit H   Supporting Documents
1. Personal resumes
2. Cost of living budget
3. Letters of reference
4. Copies of leases
5. Anything else of relevance to the plan

Exhibit I   Summary

Often, you can complete the process in 8 steps:

1. Define long-term objectives
2. State short-term goals
3. Set marketing strategies
4. Analyze available resources (personnel, material, etc.)
5. Assemble financial data
6. Review for realism
7. Rewrite
8. Implement

Defining Long-Term Objectives. Start with the objectives of your import/export business. Think ahead. What do I want the business to be like in 3 years? 5 years? 20 years? How big a business do you want?

Stating Short-term Goals. Define your import/export business in terms of sales volume and assets. Be precise; state them in measurable units of time and dollars.

Setting Marketing Strategies. If, like Teresa Brown, who is marketing bead fringe from Egypt, you have done your homework and applied the marketing concepts offered in chapter 3, this part of the business plan should be simple.

If not, go back and review the marketing section of chapter 3, because nothing will happen with your business until you make a sale. If sales aren't made, projections and other plans fall apart. Profitable sales support the business, so be prepared to spend 75% of your planning time on market efforts. Ultimately, the best marketing information comes through your own industry—here or overseas. Talk to those with experience. Talk to United States and foreign manufacturers as well as other importers/exporters. Don't overlook the data that you can find in libraries.

Make your market plan precise. Describe your competitive advantage. Outline your geographical and product-line priorities. Write down your sales goals. List your alternatives for market penetration. Will you sell direct or through agents? What is the advertising budget? Travel in an import/export business is a must. What is the travel budget? How much will it cost to expand your markets? What will be the cost of communications?

Analyzing Available Resources. Now for the pain. You must now ask yourself whether you have the resources to make the plan work. Take a management inventory. Do you have the skills to market your products? Do you need administrative or

Proforma Sales (Shipments) Projection
Fiscal Year 19xx

Product Line (s) Product (s)	Jan	Feb	March	April	May	June	July	Aug	Sept	Oct	Nov	Dec	Year
A. Product Line A													
1. Product 1													
Shipments (Units)													
X Ave. Price/Unit													
Gross Sales	$	$	$	$	$	$	$	$	$	$	$	$	$
2. Product 2													
3. Product 3													
n. Product N													
Product Line A—Gross Sales	$	$	$	$	$	$	$	$	$	$	$	$	$
B. Product Line B													
C. Product Line C													
N. Product Line N													
Total Gross Sales	$	$	$	$	$	$	$	$	$	$	$	$	$

Fig. 7-1   A sample pro forma sales projection worksheet.

accounting skills? Will you need warehouse space? Will you need translators? How much cash will you need?

Assembling Financial Data. After all the dreaming and reality testing of the first four steps, you must now express them in terms of cash flow, profit and loss projections, and balance sheets. Figure 7-1 shows a pro forma sales projection (3-year summary, detailed by month for the first year, detailed by quarter for the second and third years). Figure 7-2 is a pro forma income (profit and loss) statement (detailed by month for the first year, detailed by quarter for the second and third years). Figure 7-3 is a pro forma balance sheet, and Figure 7-4 is a pro forma cash-flow statement (detailed by month for the first year, detailed by quarter for the second and third years). This usage of *pro forma* means estimating information in advance in a prescribed form.

The cash flow and the profit and loss projections serve double duty. They quantify the sales and operating goals, including use of personnel and other resources expressed in dollars and time. As a guide to the future, you can use them as control documents and measure progress toward goals. The balance sheet shows what your business owns, what it owes, and how those assets and liabilities are distributed.

Reviewing for Realism. Your plan must not set contradictory goals. A coherent plan fits together. You cannot be expanding the introduction of goose liver from China at the same time you are getting out of animal products and into irrigation machinery. Look at your plan as a whole and ask, "Does this make good business sense?"

Rewrite. Now that the first draft is complete, let at least 10 experienced people look at it. Ask them to be critical and to tell you the truth. Let them know up front that you have a lot of ego in this project, but that because you want to be a success, you want their criticism, no matter how much it hurts.

Implementation. In the words of President (General) Dwight Eisenhower, "The plan is nothing; planning is everything." Your business plan provides a road map, but the acid test is whether it will work. Like a map, you might have to detour to get where you are going, so don't put the map on the shelf and forget about it. Use it as an operating document. Review it and revise it as experience dictates.

Now you're ready to go. You've done your homework and

Proforma Income Statement
Fiscal Year 19xx

	Jan	Feb	March	April	May	June	July	Aug	Sept	Oct	Nov	Dec	Year
Gross Sales													
less: Discounts, allowances, etc.													
Net Sales													
less: Variable costs													
Manufacturing:													
Material													
Labor													
Variable overhead													
Other													
Variable costs (manufacturing)													
Operating:													
Commissions													
Other													
Variable costs (operating)													
Variable costs (total)													
Contribution													
Percent of net sales (%)													
less: Fixed costs													
Manufacturing													
Engineering													
Selling													
General and Administrative													
Financial													
Fixed costs (total)													
Profit before taxes													
less: Taxes													
Net income													

Fig. 7-2   A sample pro forma income statement.

Proforma Balance Sheet Fiscal Year 19xx	Actual Dec	Jan	Feb	March	April	May	June	July	Aug	Sept	Oct	Nov	Dec
A. Assets Employed													
1. Current Assets													
Cash													
Accounts receivable (net)													
Inventory													
Prepaids													
Other													
Subtotal													
2. Current Liabilities													
(excluding debt)													
Accounts payable													
Accrued liabilities													
Taxes payable													
Other													
Subtotal													
Working capital (1–2)													
3. Property, Plant, and													
Equipment													
Land													
Building													
Equipment													
less: Accumulated depreciation	( )												
Subtotal													
4. Other Assets													
Investments													
Other													
Subtotal													
Assets Employed													
B. Capital Structure													
1. Debt													
Short-term Notes													
Long-term (current portion)													
Long-term Debt													
Other													
Subtotal													
2. Deferred Taxes													
3. Shareholders Equity													
Paid in Capital													
Retained Earnings													
Subtotal													
Capital Structure													

Fig. 7-3   A sample of a pro forma balance sheet.

Proforma Cash Flow Statement (Operational)
Fiscal Year 19xx

	Jan	Feb	March	April	May	June	July	Aug	Sept	Oct	Nov	Dec	Year
Cash Receipts													
Collection of accounts receivable													
Sale of assets													
Borrowings													
Equity financing													
Other													
Cash receipts													
Cash Expenditures													
Material													
Freight													
Wages and salaries													
Commissions													
Fringe benefits													
Manufacturing expenses													
Selling expenses													
General and administrative expenses													
Financial expenses													
Subtotal													
Capital expenditures													
Debt repayment													
Dividends													
Other													
Cash expenditures													
Cash Flows													
Cumulative cash flows													

Fig. 7-4   A sample of a pro forma cash flow statement.

written your business plan. If you've gotten this far, you have the style and determination to make it work.

By now, you have written your first letter and made your first contact. As an importer, you've asked for literature and samples or, as an exporter, you've sent them. You want early orders, and if you have done your homework, they should start rolling in, but be patient. Everything takes a little longer in international business.

SUCCESS STORY: Teresa Brown flies regularly to Europe and the Middle East, where she buys products with the ease of a professional buyer, which she now is. Her profits are remarkable and she has a lifestyle she designed herself.

The next chapter offers 20 tips to gain import/export success and big profits.

Twenty Ways to Win Import/Export Success

SUCCESS IN THE INTERNATIONAL MARKETPLACE IS MEASURED IN profits and market share. It is also measured in the satisfaction that you have in reaching new horizons and visiting places that previously were only dreams. You and your firm can be success-ful if you act on these 20 critical keys.

1. The most important key to success is commitment by you, the decision maker, to enter the global market.

You'll reap tax advantages, sales-volume advantages, the excitement of the international experience, and lots of profit.

Change your game and get into the global competition. Get to work and earn a share of the more than $250 billion dollars that's out there waiting for enthusiastic entreprenurial Ameri-cans.

2. Get beyond cultural obstacles.

Accept the fact that the rest of the world isn't just like the United States. They like their way of doing things, or they would change it. Get used to the idea that cultural differences exist, but be assured that you can understand and even learn the differences. At a minimum, you can appreciate and respect the differences. Remember that there are more similarities among people of the world than there are differences.

The Japanese like cars, and they don't dislike American cars. The problem is that American car manufacturers just haven't figured out how to satisfy the Japanese car consumer, who is used to a different style and, above all, different service considerations. The world is becoming more and more internationalized.

3. Plan, plan, plan, but do not treat international trade as a stand-alone process.

Plan for success. Assuming that your initial market research effort revealed some demand for your product as it is or with minor redesign, develop a strategic plan for your business. From the beginning, write out the plan. What is your competitive advantage? What are your geographical and product line priorities? How are you going to penetrate the market?

4. The market, the market, the market.

An early investigation of the market is the key that leads to success. Get an estimate of the demand for the products that you already manufacture. The best information will come from your own industry—here and overseas. Talk to those who have experience. Don't overlook available statistics and library resources. Lay out a map of the world and apply some logic. If you plan to export, divide the world into export regions and prioritize the regions based on broad assumptions of their need for your product and their ability to pay. Based on your common understanding of the various countries, regions, their languages, the environment, and their cultures, select one or more target countries for start-up. Do consider the political and financial stability of the country. Use the same logic for imports. Examine a map of the United States or your region, and divide the map into target segments. Do not try to sell to all of America, the entire world, or even one entire foreign country immediately, but remember that nothing happens until you sell something.

5. Information is critical.

Research is critical to the success of your market plan. Begin with a list of the information you will need to support your analysis. What do you need to know about the regions of the United States (imports) or the foreign country (exports) you have selected? What level of detail will you require? Next, organize a list of the potential sources of your research. Classify your sources and begin the process of doing a logical sort of the material. You can gain the most accurate and meaningful information by traveling to the potential market.

6. What are your market goals?

Develop a well-researched, solidly-reasoned market plan. It should include a background review, an analysis of the market environment, and a description of your goals in terms of your company.

7. Where there are competitors, there is a market.

Take a close look at the competition. It will be to your favor to discover that there is competition. Why? Because, where there is competition, there is a market!!

8. Persistence—don't give up.

Don't become discouraged if you find that your product is ahead of its time in the international marketplace. Don't give up on exporting. WD-40 and Coca-Cola created a global market for their product. Search for products that do have an overseas market and are similar to yours.

9. Adapt the product to the market.

Learn what products your market likes and how they like the products, whether you are importing an article for American tastes or exporting a product for a foreign market. Be ready to adapt your product to the market. Redesign your product and compete.

10. Budget for success.

Include international goals in your financial plan. Treat import/export start-up as you would any other entrepreneurial venture. Budget from the beginning and keep good books. Watch your costs and cash flow. Like any new business, expect short-term losses, but plan for long-term gains.

11. You gotta manage.

Manage for success. Develop the tactical plans that implement your overall strategic plan, such as a personnel plan, an advertising policy, a market entry, and a sales approach. Motivate your personnel by emphasizing teamwork.

12. Be patient; international trade takes a little longer.

International trade takes a little longer than domestic trade. After all, oceans are in between, and the transportation systems are slower. Every transaction will require financing. International financing and banking methods are sophisticated and generally excellent, but negotiations and transactions across borders take more time than domestic business.

13. The best long-term investment is a well-planned trip.

Those things go right that the boss checks. In international business, that means international travel. After you have developed your strategic plan, visit the overseas sources or markets you have chosen. There is nothing like getting first-hand information. You will find it interesting, rewarding, and essential to meet the people with whom you will be doing business. Even after you have established a successful sales and distribution network, it is necessary that you, or representatives of your company, visit them at least twice a year.

14. Walk on two legs.

Choose carefully a good international banker, freight forwarder, and customhouse broker. Talk with them to learn the language of international business—pricing, quotations, shipping, and getting paid. Establish a good relationship, then stick with it. Deal with a bank that has personnel who are experienced in the international marketplace.

15. Proper communication gets sales results.

Provide customer service the international way—by communicating often, clearly, and simply. Keep your overseas business partners on the team by being particularly sensitive to communications, letters, telexes, and phone calls.

16. Expert counsel saves money.

Minimize your inevitable mistakes by asking for help. Banks, customhouse brokers, freight forwarders, and the

United States Department of Commerce are sources of free information. Most private consultants ask reasonable fees also.

17. Selection of distributors is critical.

Your objective is to get your product in front of your buyer—decision-making units (DMU). The wrong distributor can stifle your market efforts and tie you up legally.

18. Stick to a marketing strategy

Don't chase orders. Of course, fill the over-the-counter orders, but be proactive rather than reactive. Establish an effective marketing effort according to your market plan.

19. Treat international partners and customers the same as domestic counterparts.

It might surprise some people that the foreign ratio is less than half of the United States bad-debt ratio. The reason is that in the United States, credit is a way of life. In overseas markets, credit is still something to be earned as a result of having a record of prompt payment. Use common sense in extending credit to overseas customers, but don't use tougher rules than for your American clients.

20. Don't fret about the international business cycle.

Don't worry about booms or busts, just do it. International trade is exciting and profitable because there are so many side benefits. Think of traveling to such exotic places as Hong Kong or Vienna and writing off the trip as an expense to the company.

Ok, you've found the sources, developed the markets, written the business plan, and have the entrepreneurial spirit to make your own import/export business a success.

The time to get into the import/export market is now!!!

Appendix A
Foreign Business Organizations

All countries have the business organization known in the United States as the corporation. Some foreign countries further differentiate according to whether these companies are privately or publicly held. Here are examples of common overseas organizations:

Britain	Limited Liability Company (Ltd.)
France	Societe Anonume (S.A.) (SARL)
Hong Kong	Limited Liability Company (Ltd.)
	Private Limited Company (Pte. Ltd.)
Malaysia	Berhad (Bhd)
	Sindrian Berhad (Sdn. Bhd.)
Singapore	Limited Liability Company (Ltd.)
	Private Limited Company (Pte. Ltd.)
Spain	Sociadad Anonima (S.A.)
West Germany	Aktiengeselschaft (A.G.)
	Gesellschaft mit beschraenkter Huftung (GmbH)

Appendix B
Foreign Commercial Services Overseas Posts

The International Trade Administration (ITA) of the Department of Commerce keeps offices in the United States embassies of the countries listed below. When visiting one of these countries, you would be wise, as one of your first stops, to visit the officer posted to the office as part of the United States Foreign Commercial Service (FCS). They are there to help you do business.

*DENOTES REGIONAL OFFICE WITH SUPERVISORY REGIONAL RESPONSIBILITIES
•DENOTES TRADE SPECIALIST AT A BRANCH OFFICE

WESTERN HEMISPHERE

Argentina
Buenos Aires

Bolivia
La Paz

Brazil
Brasilia
Porto Alegre
Rio De Janeiro
Salvador
Sao Paulo

Canada
Ottawa
Calgary
Montreal
Toronto
Vancouver

Chile
Santiago

Colombia
Bogota

Costa Rica
San Jose

Dominican Republic
Santo Domingo

Ecuador
Quito
Guayaquil

Guatemala
Guatemala City

Honduras
Tegucigalpa

Mexico
Mexico, D.F.
Monterrey
Guadalajara

Panama
Panama City

Peru
Lima

Uruguay
Montevideo

Venezuela
Caracas

AFRICA/NEAR EAST/SOUTH ASIA

Algeria
Algiers

Cameroon
Yaounde
Douala

Egypt
Cairo
Alexandria

Ghana
Accra

India
New Delhi
Bombay
Calcutta
Madras

Iraq
Baghdad

Israel
Tel Aviv

Ivory Coast
Abidjan

Kenya
Nairobi

Kuwait
Kuwait City

Liberia
Monrovia

Morocco
Rabat
Casablanca

Nigeria
Lagos
Kaduna

Pakistan
Karachi
Lahore

Saudi Arabia
Jidda
Dhahran
Riyadh

South Africa
Johannesburg

United Arab Emirates
Abu Dhabi
Dubai

Zaire
Kinshasa

Zimbabwe
Harare

EUROPE

Austria
Vienna

Belgium
Brussels
Antwerp

Czechoslovakia
Prague

Denmark
Copenhagen

Finland
Helsinki

France
Paris
Bordeaux
Lyon
Marseille
Strasbourg

Germany
Bonn
Berlin (West)
Dusseldorf
Frankfurt
Hamburg
Munich
Stuttgart

Greece
Athens
Thessaloniki

Hungary
Budapest

Italy
Rome
Florence
Genoa
Milan
Naples
Palermo

Netherlands
The Hague
Amsterdam
Rotterdam

Norway
Oslo

Poland
Warsaw

Portugal
Lisbon
Oporto

Romania
Bucharest

Spain
Madrid
Barcelona

Sweden
Stockholm

Switzerland
Bern
Zurich

Turkey
Ankara
Istanbul

United Kingdom
London

U.S.S.R.
Moscow

Yugoslavia
Belgrade
Zagreb

EAST ASIA AND THE PARCIFIC

Australia
Canberra
Melbourne
Perth
Sydney

China
Beijing
Guangzhou
Shanghai

Hong Kong
Hong Kong

Indonesia
Jakarta
Surabaya

Japan
Tokyo
Fukuoka
Osaka-Kobe
Sapporo

Korea
Seoul

Malaysia
Kuala Lumpur

New Zealand
Wellington
Auckland

Phillippines
Manila

Singapore
Singapore City

Thailand
Bangkok

Note: For information about U.S. and Foreign Commercial Service Posts call 202-377-1599.

Appendix C
District Offices of the U.S. International Trade Administration

In the United States, the International Trade Administration (ITA), a division of the Commerce Department, keeps offices in the cities listed below. The staffs of these offices are there to help you do international business.

ALABAMA
*Birmingham—Rm. 302, 2015 2nd Ave. North, Berry Bldg., 35203 (205) 731-1331

ALASKA
Anchorage—701 C St., P.O. Box 32, 99513, (907) 271-5041

ARIZONA
Phoenix—Federal Bldg. & U.S. Courthouse, 230 North 1st Ave., Rm. 3412, 85025, (602) 261-3285

ARKANSAS
Little Rock—Suite 811, Savers Fed. Bldg., 320 W. Capitol Ave., 72201, (501) 378-5794

CALIFORNIA
Los Angeles—Rm. 800, 11777 San Vicente Blvd., 90049, (213) 209-6707
*Santa Ana—116-A W. 4th St., Suite #1, 92701, (714) 836-2461
San Diego—6363 Greenwich Dr., 92122, (619) 293-5395
*San Francisco—Fed. Bldg., Box 36013, 450 Golden Gate Ave., 94102, (415) 556-5860

COLORADO
*Denver—Rm. 119, U.S. Customhouse, 721-19th St., 80202, (303) 844-3246

CONNECTICUT
*Hartford—Rm. 610-B, Fed. Office Bldg., 450 Main St., 06103, (203) 240-3530

DELAWARE
Serviced by Philadelphia District Office

DISTRICT OF COLUMBIA
*Washington, D.C.—(Baltimore, Md. District) Rm. 1066 HCHB, Department of Commerce, 14th St. & Constitution Ave., N.W. 20230, (202) 377-3181

FLORIDA
Miami—Suite 224, Fed. Bldg., 51 S.W. First Ave., 33130, (305) 536-5267
*Clearwater—128 North Osceola Ave. 33515, (813) 461-0011
*Jacksonville—1200 Gulf Life Dr., S. #104, 32207, (904) 791-2796
*Orlando—75 East Ivanhoe Blvd., 32804, (305) 425-1234
*Tallahassee—Collins Bldg., Rm. 401, 107 W. Gaines St., 32304, (904) 488-6469

GEORGIA
Atlanta—Suite 504, 1365 Peachtree St., N.E., 30309, (404) 347-4872
Savannah—120 Barnard St., A-107, 31402, (912) 944-4204

HAWAII
Honolulu—4106 Fed. Bldg., P.O. Box 50026, 300 Ala Moana Blvd., 96850, (808) 541-1782

IDAHO
*Boise—(Denver, Colorado District) Statehouse, Room 113, 837200, (208) 334 – 9254

ILLINOIS
Chicago—1406 Mid Continental Plaza Bldg., 55 East Monroe St., 60603, (312) 353-4450
*Palatine—W.R. Harper College, Algonquin & Rosele Rd., 60067, (312) 397-3000, x-532
*Rockford—515 North Court St., P.O. Box 1747, 61110-0247, (815) 987-8100

INDIANA
Indianapolis—357 U.S. Courthouse & Fed. Office Bldg., 46 East Ohio St., 46204, (317) 269-6214

IOWA
Des Moines—817 Fed. Bldg., 210 Walnut St., 50309, (515) 284-4222

KANSAS
*Wichita—(Kansas City, Missouri District) River Park Pl., Suite 565, 727 North Waco, 67203, (316) 269-6160

KENTUCKY
Louisville—Rm. 636B, U.S. Post Office and Courthouse Bldg., 40202, (502) 582-5066

LOUISIANA
New Orleans—432 World Trade Center, No. 2 Canal St., 70130, (504) 589-6546

MAINE
*Augusta—(Boston, Massachusetts District) 1 Memorial Circle, Casco Bank Bldg., 04330, (207) 622-8249

MARYLAND
Baltimore—415 U.S. Customhouse, Gay and Lombard Sts. 21202, (301) 962-3560

MASSACHUSETTS
Boston—World Trade Center, Suite 307 Commonwealth Pier Area, 02210, (617) 565-8563

MICHIGAN
Detroit—1140 McNamara Bldg., 477 Michigan Ave., 48226, (313) 226-3650
*Grand Rapids—300 Monroe N.W., Rm. 409, 49503, (616) 456-2411

MINNESOTA
Minneapolis—108 Fed. Bldg., 110 S. 4th St., 55401, (612) 348-1638

MISSISSIPPI
Jackson—328 Jackson Mall Office Center, 300 Woodrow Wilson Blvd., 39213, (601) 965-4388

MISSOURI
*St. Louis—7911 Forsyth Blvd., Suite 610, 63105, (314) 425-3302-4
Kansas City—Rm. 635, 601 East 12th St., 64106, (816) 374-3141

MONTANA
Serviced by Denver District Office

NEBRASKA
Omaha—11133 "O" St., 68137, (402) 221-3664

NEVADA
Reno—1755 E. Plumb Ln., #152, 89502, (702) 784-5203

NEW HAMPSHIRE
Serviced by Boston District Office

NEW JERSEY
*Trenton—3131 Princeton Pike Bldg. 4D, Suite 211, 98648, (609) 989-2100

NEW MEXICO
Albuquerque—517 Gold, S.W., Suite 4303, 87102, (505) 766-2386

NEW YORK
Buffalo—1312 Fed. Bldg., 111 West Huron St., 14202, (716) 846-4191
*Rochester—121 East Ave., 14604, (716) 263-6480
New York—Fed. Office Bldg., 26 Fed Plaza, Foley Sq., 10278, (212) 264-0634

NORTH CAROLINA
*Greensboro—324 W. Market St., P.O. Box 1950, 27402, (919) 333-5345

NORTH DAKOTA
Serviced by Omaha District Office

OHIO
*Cincinnati—9504 Fed. Office Bldg., 550 Main St., 45202, (513) 684-2944
Cleveland—Rm. 600, 666 Euclid Ave., 44114 (216) 522-4750

OKLAHOMA
Oklahoma City—5 Broadway Executive Park, Suite 200, 6601 Broadway Extension, 73116, (405) 231-5302
*Tulsa—440 S. Houston St., 74127, (918) 581-7650

OREGON
Portland—Rm. 618, 1220 S.W. 3rd Ave., 97204, (503) 221-3001

PENNSYLVANIA
Philadelphia—9448 Fed. Bldg., 600 Arch St., 19106 (215) 597-2866
Pittsburgh—2002 Fed. Bldg., 1000 Liberty Ave., 15222, (412) 644-2850

PUERTO RICO
San Juan (Hato Rey)—Rm. 659-Fed. Bldg., 00918, (809) 753-4555

RHODE ISLAND
*Providence—(Boston, Massachusetts District) 7 Jackson Walkway, 02903, (401) 528-5104, ext. 22

SOUTH CAROLINA
Columbia—Strom Thurmond Fed. Bldg., Suite 172, 1835 Assembly St., 29201 (803) 765-5345
*Charleston—17 Lockwood Dr., 29401, (803) 724-4361

SOUTH DAKOTA
Serviced by Omaha District Office

TENNESSEE
Nashville—Suite 1114, Parkway Towers, 404 James Robertson Parkway, 37219-1505, (615) 736-5161
*Memphis—555 Beale St., 38103, (901) 521-4137

TEXAS
*Dallas—Rm. 7A5, 1100 Commerce St., 75242, (214) 767-0542
*Austin—P.O. Box 12728, Capitol Station, 78711, (512) 472-5059
Houston—2625 Fed. Courthouse, 515 Rusk St., 77002, (713) 229-2578

UTAH
Salt Lake City—Rm. 340 U.S. Courthouse, 350 S. Main St., 84101, (801) 524-5116

VERMONT
Serviced by Boston District Office

VIRGINIA
Richmond—8010 Fed. Bldg., 400 North 8th St., 23240, (804) 771-2246

WASHINGTON
Seattle—3131 Elliott Ave., Suite 290, 98121, (206) 442-5616
*Spokane—P.O. Box 2170, 99210 (509) 456-4557

WEST VIRGINIA
Charleston—3309 New Fed. Bldg., 500 Quarrier St., 25301, (304) 347-5123

WISCONSIN
Milwaukee—Fed. Bldg., U.S. Courthouse, 517 E. Wisc. Ave., 53202, (414) 291-3473

WYOMING
Serviced by Denver District Office

Appendix D
Customs Service Organization

The listings on this page and the next show how the United States Customs Department is organized and who to contact on matters related to importing your goods into the United States.

		COMMISSIONER OF CUSTOMS William von Raab (202) 566-2101 DEPUTY COMMISSIONER Michael H. Lane (202) 566-2145	COMMISSIONER'S STAFF Mieko Kosobayashi Confidential Assistant (202) 566-2101 D. Lynn Gordon Executive Assistant to the Commissioner (202) 566-9161 Charles Parkinson, Associate Commissioner Congressional and Public Affairs (202) 566-9102 David Gencarelli Director Congressional Affairs (202) 566-5644 Dennis H. Murphy Director Public Affairs (202) 566-5286 Earl M. Mitchell Special Assistant to the Commissioner (Equal Opportunity) (202) 535-9002	CHIEF COUNSEL Michael T. Schmitz (202) 566-5476 COMPTROLLER William F. Riley (Acting) (202) 566-2416 ASSISTANT COMMISSIONERS: ENFORCEMENT William Rosenblatt (202) 566-2416 INTERNATIONAL AFFAIRS James W. Shaver (202) 566-5303 INSPECTION & CONTROL Samuel H. Banks (202) 566-2366 COMMERCIAL OPERATIONS Gerald McManus (202) 566-5497 INTERNAL AFFAIRS William Green (202) 566-8518

REGIONAL OFFICERS	NORTHEAST	NEW YORK	SOUTHEAST	SOUTH CENTRAL	SOUTHWEST	PACIFIC	NORTH CENTRAL
Addresses	10 Causeway St. BOSTON MA 02222-1059	6 World Trade Ct. NEW YORK NY 10048	99 S.E. 5th St. MIAMI FL 33131	423 Canal St. NEW ORLEANS LA 70130	5850 San Felipe St. HOUSTON TX 77057	300 N. Los Angeles St. LOS ANGELES CA 90053 (213) 894-5901	55 E. Monroe St. CHICAGO IL 60603-5790
Regional Commissioner	Vacant (617) 565-6210	Edward E. Kwas (212) 466-4444	George Heavey (305) 536-5952	J. Robert Grimes (504) 589-6324	James Piatt (Acting) (713) 953-6843	Quintin L. Villaneuva, Jr. (213) 894-5901	Richard McMullen (312) 353-6250
Asst. Regional Commissioner (Operations)	Edward A. Goggin (617) 565-6240	Anthony Liberta (212) 466-4487	Garnett Fee (305) 536-5952	David P. Banowetz (504) 589-6476	Tom Blanchard (Acting) (713) 953-6843	Robert Trotter (213) 894-5901	James Piatt (312) 353-8002
Regional Counsel	John deRomoet (617) 565-6350	Melvin N. Minsky (212) 466-4562	Stuart P. Seidel (305) 536-4321	James M. Moster (504) 589-6981	David P. Lindsey (713) 953-6827	Paul E. Wilson (213) 894-5936	Saul N. Perla (312) 353-7860
Regional Director Internal Affairs	William Rudman (617) 565-5950	Anthony L. Dondrea, Jr. (212) 466-5928	Charles C. Mantle (305) 536-5306	Ronald R. Bernhard (504) 589-2187	Kenneth E. McNamara (713) 953-6989	Robert D. Maloof (213) 894-2564	
Asst. Regional Commissioner (Enforcement)	Donald S. Donohue (617) 565-6251	David J. Ripa (212) 466-5641	Leon Guinn (Acting) (305) 536-5952	Larry LaDage (Acting) (504) 589-6499	John A. Burns (713) 953-6843	John E. Hensley (213) 894-4692	Donald Watson (312) 886-9596
Public Affairs Officer	Edward V. Callanan (617) 565-6215	Janet Rapaport (212) 466-4547	Clifton V. Stallings (305) 536-4126	Liz Orgeron (504) 589-2976	Charles W. Conroy (713) 953-6905	Mike Fleming (213) 894-5939	Cherise Mayberry (312) 886-3377

Appendix E
U.S. Customs Districts

(Note: New York and Minnesota have Area Directors instead of District Directors)

Region	District	Phone	Director
Pac.	Anchorage, Alaska 99501 / 620 E. Tenth Ave., Suite 101	(907) 271-4043	Duane Oveson
N.E.	Baltimore, Maryland 21202 / 40 S. Gay St.	(301) 962-2666	A. Robert Beikirch
N.E.	Boston, Massachusetts 02222-1059 / 10 Causeway St.	(617) 565-6147	John V. Linde
N.E.	Buffalo, New York 14202 / 111 W. Huron St.	(716) 846-4374	Carlton L. Brainard
S.E.	Charleston, South Carolina 29402 / 200 E. Bay St.	(803) 724-4312	William Byrd
S.E.	Charlotte Amalie, St. Thomas-Virgin Islands 00801 / Main P.O. Sugar Estate	(809) 774-2530	Ralph C. Muser
N.Cen.	Chicago, Illinois 60607 / 610 S. Canal St.	(312) 353-6100	Richard Roster
N.Cen.	Cleveland, Ohio 44114 / 55 Erieview Plaza	(216) 522-4284	John F. Nelson
S.W.	Dallas/Fort Worth, Texas 75261 / 700 Parkway Plaza, P.O. Box 619050	(214) 574-2170	David Greenleaf
N.Cen.	Detroit, Michigan 48226 / 477 Michigan Ave.	(313) 226-3177	William L. Morandini
N.Cen.	Duluth, Minnesota 55802-1390 / 515 W. First St., 209 Fed. Bldg.	(218) 720-5201	Robert W. Nordness
S.W.	El Paso, Texas 79985 / Bldg. B, Room 134 Bridge of the Americas P.O. Box 9516	(915) 534-6799	Mike Mach
N.Cen.	Great Falls, Montana 59401 / 600 Central Plaza, Suite 200	(406) 453-7631	Don W. Myhra
Pac.	Honolulu, Hawaii 96806 / 335 Merchant St. / P.O. Box 1641	(808) 541-1725	George Roberts
S.W.	Houston/Galveston, Texas 77052 / 701 San Jacinto St., P.O. Box 52790	(713) 226-2334	Patricia McCauley
S.W.	Laredo, Texas 78041-3130 / Mann Rd. & Santa Maria P.O. Box 3130	(512) 726-2267	Joseph Castellano
Pac.	Los Angeles/Long Beach, California / 300 S. Ferry St., Terminal Island 90731	(213) 514-6001	John Heinrich
S.E.	Miami, Florida 33131 / 77 S.E. 5th St.	(305) 536-4101	Harry W. Carnes
N.Cen.	Milwaukee, Wisconsin 53202 / 517 E. Wisconsin Ave.	(414) 291-3924	Richard L. Rudin
N.Cen.	Minneapolis, Minnesota 55401 / 110 S. Fourth St.	(612) 348-1690	Robert W. Nordness
S.Cen.	Mobile, Alabama 36652 / 250 N. Water St. / P.O. Box 2748	(205) 690-2106	David L. Willett
S.Cen.	New Orleans, Louisiana 70130 / 423 Canal St.	(504) 589-6353	Joel R. Mish
N.Y.	New York, New York		
	New York Seaport Area, New York, New York 10048 Customhouse, 6 World Trade Center	(212) 466-5817	Peter J. Baish
	Kennedy Airport Area, Jamaica, New York 11430 Cargo Bldg. 80, Room 2E	(718) 917-1542	John J. Martuge
	Newark Area, Newark, New Jersey 07114 Airport International Plaza	(201) 645-3760	Max G. Willis
S.W.	Nogales, Arizona 85621 / International & Terrace Sts., P.O. Box 670	(602) 287-9163	Peter F. Gonzalez
S.E.	Norfolk, Virginia 23510 / 101 E. Main St.	(804) 441-6546	Phil Spayd
N.E.	Ogdensburg, New York, 13669 / 127 N. Water St.	(315) 393-0660	William Dietzel
N.Cen.	Pembina, North Dakota 58271 / Post Office Bldg.	(701) 825-6201	Raymond J. Hagerty, Jr.
N.E.	Philadelphia, Pennsylvania 19106 / 2nd & Chestnut Sts., Room 102	(215) 597-4605	Anthony Piazza
S.W.	Port Arthur, Texas 77642 / 4550 75th St.	(409) 724-0087	Richard J. Garcia
N.E.	Portland, Maine 04112 / 312 Fore St., P.O. Box 4688	(207) 780-3326	Emery W. Ingalls
Pac.	Portland, Oregon 97209 / 511 N.W. Broadway	(503) 221-2865	Clyde Kellay, Jr.
N.E.	Providence, Rhode Island 02903 / 24 Weybosset St.	(401) 528-5080	Philip Bernard (Acting)
N.E.	St. Albans, Vermont 05478 / Main & Stebbins St., P.O. Box 111	(802) 524-6572/8	Frank R. Spendley
N.Cen.	St. Louis, Missouri 63105 / 7911 Forsyth Bldg., Suite 625	(314) 425-3134	Theodore Galantowicz
Pac.	San Diego, California 92188 / 880 Front St., Suite 559	(619) 557-5360	Allan J. Rappoport
Pac.	San Francisco, California 94126 / 555 Battery St., P.O. Box 2450	(415) 556-4340	Paul Andrews
S.E.	San Juan, Puerto Rico 00903 / P.O. Box 2112	(809) 723-2091	Mamie E. Pollock
S.E.	Savannah, Georgia 31401 / 1 East Bay St.	(912) 944-4256	Robert J. Richter
Pac.	Seattle, Washington 98174 / 909 First Ave.	(206) 442-0554	Daniel C. Holland
S.E.	Tampa, Florida 33602 / 301 S. Ashley Dr.	(813) 228-2381	Diane Zwicker
S.E.	Washington, D.C. 20041 / POB 17423 Gateway 1 Bldg., Dulles Intl. Apt., Chantilly, Va. 22021	(202) 566-8511	Sidney A. Reyes
S.E.	Wilmington, North Carolina 28401 / One Virginia Ave.	(919) 343-4601	James Mahony

Appendix F
United States Government Bookstores

You can purchase many valuable books and publications at very reasonable prices through the United States Government Bookstore. Check below to learn the location of the store nearest you.

GPO operates 24 bookstores all around the country where you can browse through the shelves and take your books home with you. Naturally, these stores can't stock all of the more than 16,000 titles in our inventory, but they do carry the ones you're most likely to be looking for. And they'll be happy to special order any Government book currently offered for sale. All of our bookstores accept VISA, Choice, MasterCard, and Superintendent of Documents deposit account orders.

ALABAMA
O'Neill Building
2021 Third Ave., North
Birmingham, Alabama 35203
(205) 731-1056
9:00 AM–5:00 PM

CALIFORNIA
ARCO Plaza, C-Level
505 South Flower Street
Los Angeles, California 90071
(213) 894-5841
8:30 AM–4:30 PM

Room 1023, Federal Building
450 Golden Gate Avenue
San Francisco, California 94102
(415) 556-0643
8:00 AM–4:00 PM

COLORADO
Room 117, Federal Building
1961 Stout Street
Denver, Colorado 80294
(303) 844-3964
8:00 AM–4:00 PM

World Savings Building
720 North Main Street
Pueblo, Colorado 81003
(303) 544-3142
9:00 AM–5:00 PM

DISTRICT OF COLUMBIA
U.S. Government Printing Office
710 North Capitol Street
Washington, DC 20401
(202) 275-2091
8:00 AM–4:00 PM

Commerce Department
Room 1604, 1st Floor
14th & Penn., NW, South Side
Washington, DC 20230
(202) 377-3527
8:00 AM–4:00 PM

Farragut West
1510 H Street, NW
Washington, DC 20005
(202) 653-5075
9:00 AM–5:00 PM

FLORIDA
Room 158, Federal Building
400 W. Bay Street
Jacksonville, Florida 32202
(904) 791-3801
8:00 AM–4:00 PM

GEORGIA
Room 100, Federal Building
275 Peachtree Street, NE
P.O. Box 56445
Atlanta, Georgia 30343
(404) 331-6947
8:00 AM–4:00 PM

ILLINOIS
Room 1365, Federal Building
219 S. Dearborn Street
Chicago, Illinois 60604
(312) 353-5133
8:00 AM–4:00 PM

MASSACHUSETTS
Room G25, Federal Building
Sudbury Street
Boston, Massachusetts 02203
(617) 565-2488
8:00 AM–4:00 PM

MICHIGAN
Suite 160, Federal Building
477 Michigan Avenue
Detroit, Michigan 48226
(313) 226-7816
8:00 AM–4:00 PM

MISSOURI
120 Bannister Mall
5600 E. Bannister Road
Kansas City, Missouri 64137
(816) 765-2256
Mon–Sat 10:00 AM–9:30 PM
Sun 12:00 Noon–6:00 PM

NEW YORK
Room 110
26 Federal Plaza
New York, New York 10278
(212) 264-3825
8:00 AM–4:00 PM

OHIO
1st Floor, Federal Building
1240 E. 9th Street
Cleveland, Ohio 44199
(216) 522-4922
9:00 AM–5:00 PM

Room 207, Federal Building
200 N. High Street
Columbus, Ohio 43215
(614) 469-6956
9:00 AM–5:00 PM

PENNSYLVANIA
Robert Morris Building
100 North 17th Street
Philadelphia, Pennsylvania 19103
(215) 597-0677
8:00 AM–4:00 PM

Room 118, Federal Building
1000 Liberty Avenue
Pittsburgh, Pennsylvania 15222
(412) 644-2721
8:30 AM–4:30 PM

TEXAS
Room 1C46, Federal Building
1100 Commerce Street
Dallas, Texas 75242
(214) 767-0076
7:45 AM–4:15 PM

9319 Gulf Freeway
Houston Texas 77017
(713) 229-3515
Mon–Sat 10:00 AM–6:00 PM

WASHINGTON
Room 194, Federal Building
915 Second Avenue
Seattle, Washington 98174
(206) 442-4270
8:00 AM–4:00 PM

WISCONSIN
Room 190, Federal Building
517 E. Wisconsin Avenue
Milwaukee, Wisconsin 53202
(414) 291-1304
8:00 AM–4:00 PM

RETAIL SALES OUTLET
8660 Cherry Lane
Laurel, Maryland 20707
(301) 953-7974
792-0262
7:45 AM–3:45 PM

All stores with the exception of Houston and Kansas City are open Mon-Fri (Houston, Mon-Sat; Kansas City, 7 days a week).

Glossary

acceptance The act of a drawee acknowledging in writing on the face of a draft payable at a fixed or determinable future date, that he will pay the draft at maturity.

acceptance draft A sight draft document against acceptance. *See* SIGHT DRAFT. DOCUMENTS AGAINST ACCEPTANCE.

ad valorem Literally, according-to-value. *See* DUTY.

advisory capacity A term indicating that a shipper's agent or representative is not empowered to make definitive decisions or adjustments without approval of the group or individual represented. *Compare* WITHOUT RESERVE.

affreightment (contract of) An agreement between steamship line (or similar carrier) and an importer or exporter in which cargo space is reserved on a vessel for a specified time and at a specified price. The importer/exporter is obligated to make payment whether or not the shipment is made.

after date A phrase indicating that payment on a draft or other negotiable instrument is due a specified number of days after presentation of the draft to the drawee or payee. *Compare* AFTER DATE, AT SIGHT.

after sight A phrase indicating that the date of maturity of a draft or other negotiable instrument is fixed by the date on which it was drawn a specified number of days after presentation of the draft to the drawee or payee. *Compare* with AFTER SIGHT, AT SIGHT.

agent *See* REPRESENTATIVE.

A.I.D. (Agency for International Development) A United States Government institution which administers economic aid to foreign countries, makes long-term loans for expansion programs in less-developed countries, and guarantees loans made by private enterprise. These loans often provide the funds to pay for United States products.

air waybill The carrying agreement between shipper and air carrier which is obtained from the airline used to ship the goods. Technically, it is a nonnegotiable instrument of air transportation which serves as a receipt for the shipper, indicating that the carrier has accepted the goods listed therein and obligates itself to carry the consignment to the airport of destination according to specified conditions. *Compare* INLAND BILL OF LADING, OCEAN BILL OF LADING, THROUGH BILL OF LADING.

alongside A phrase referring to the side of a ship. Goods to be delivered alongside are to be placed on the dock or lighter within reach of the transport ship's tackle so that they can be loaded aboard the ship.

antidiversion clause *See* DESTINATION CONTROL STATEMENT.

arbitrage The process of buying foreign exchange, stocks, bonds, and other commodities in one market and immediately selling them in another market at higher prices.

all risks clause An insurance provision which provides additional coverage to an Open Cargo Policy usually for an additional premium. Contrary to its name, the clause does not protect against all risks. The more common perils it does cover are theft, pilferage, nondelivery, fresh water damage, contact with other cargo, breakage and leakage, inherent vice, loss of market, and losses caused by delay are not covered.

amendment—letter of credit A change in the terms, amount, or expiration date of a letter of credit.

ATA Admission Temporary Admission.

ATA Carnet A customs document which enables one to carry or send goods temporarily into certain foreign countries without paying duties or posting bonds.

at sight A phrase indicating that payment on a draft or other negotiable instrument is due upon presentation or demand. *Compare* AFTER SIGHT, AFTER DATE.

authority to pay A document comparable to a revocable letter of credit but under whose terms the authority to pay the seller stems from the buyer rather than from a bank.

balance of trade The balance between a country's exports and imports.

banker's bank A bank that is established by mutual consent by independent and unaffiliated banks to provide a clearinghouse for financial transactions.

barratry Negligence or fraud on the part of a ship's officers or crew resulting in loss to the owners. *See* OPEN CARGO POLICY.

barter Trade in which merchandise is exchanged directly for other merchandise without use of money. Barter is an important means of trade with countries using currency that is not readily convertible.

beneficiary The person in whose favor a letter of credit is issued or a draft is drawn.

bill of exchange *See* DRAFT.

bill of lading A document which provides the terms of the contract between the shipper and the transportation company to move freight between stated points at a specified charge.

blanket policy *See* OPEN POLICY.

blocked exchange Exchange which cannot be freely converted into other currencies.

bonded warehouse A building authorized by customs authorities for the storage of goods without payment of duties until removal.

booking An arrangement with a steamship company for the acceptance and carriage of freight.

broker *See* EXPORT BROKER.

Brussels Tariff Nomenclature *See* NOMENCLATURE OF THE CUSTOMS COOPERATION COUNCIL.

buying agent An agent who buys in this country for foreign importers, especially for such large foreign users as mines, railroads, governments, and public utilities. Synonymous with "purchasing agent"

cash against documents (c.a.d.) Payment for goods in which a commission house or other intermediary transfers title documents to the buyer upon payment in cash.

cash in advance (c.i.a.) Payment for goods in which the price is paid in full before shipment is made. This method usually is used only for small purchases or when the goods are built.

cash with order (c.w.o.) Payment for goods in which the buyer pays when ordering and in which the transaction is binding on both parties.

carnet *See* ATA CARNET.

carrier A transportation line that hauls cargo.

CCCN (The Customs Cooperation Council Nomenclature) The customs tariff used by many countries worldwide. It is also known as the Brussels Tariff Nomenclature. *Compare* STANDARD INDUSTRIAL CLASSIFICATION, STANDARD INTERNATIONAL TRADE CLASSIFICATION, TARIFF SCHEDULE, COMMODITY GROUPINGS.

certificate of free sale A certificate, required by some foreign governments, stating that the goods for export, if products under the jurisdiction of the United States Federal Food and Drug Administration, are acceptable for sale in the United States, i.e. that the products are sold freely without restriction. FDA will issue shippers a "letter of comment" to satisfy foreign requests or regulations.

certificate of inspection A document in which certification is made as to the good condition of the merchandise immediately prior to shipment. The buyer usually designates the inspecting organization, usually an independent inspection firm or governmental body.

certificate of manufacture A statement by a producer sometimes notarized, which certifies that manufacture has been completed and that the goods are at the disposal of the buyer.

certificate of origin A document in which certification is made as to the country of origin of the merchandise.

chamber of commerce An association of businessmen whose purpose is to promote commercial and industrial interests in the community.

charter party A written contract, usually on a special form, between the owner of a vessel and a charterer who rents use of the vessel or a part of its freight space. The contract generally includes the freight rates and the ports involved in the transportation.

c & f (cost and freight) A pricing term indicating that these costs are included in the quoted price. Same as C.I.F., except that insurance is covered by the buyer.

c & i (cost and insurance) A pricing term indicating that these costs are included in the quoted price.

c.i.f. (cost, insurance, and freight) A pricing term under which the seller pays all expenses involved in the placing of merchandise on board a carrier and in addition prepays the freight and insures the goods to an agreed destination.

c.i.f. & c. (cost, insurance, freight, and commission) A pricing term indicating that these costs are included in the price.

c.i.f. & e. (cost, insurance, freight, and (currency) exchange) A pricing term indicating that these costs are included in the price.

Clayton Act A major United States antitrust law passed in 1914 to supplement the Sherman Act. The Clayton Act deals primarily with the prohibition of price discrimination among buyers by sellers in the sale of commodities and certain corporate mergers where the effect might be to substantially lessen competition or tend to create a monopoly.

clean bill of lading A bill of lading signed by the transportation company indicating that the shipment has been received in good condition with no irregularities in the packing or general condition of all or any part of the shipment. *See* FOUL BILL OF LADING.

clean draft A draft to which no documents have been attached.

collection The procedure involved in a bank's collecting money for a seller against a draft drawn on a buyer abroad, usually through a correspondent bank.

collection papers All documents (invoices, bills of lading, etc) submitted to a buyer for the purpose of receiving payment for a shipment.

collection papers The documents submitted, usually with a draft or against a letter of credit, for payment of an export shipment.

commercial attache The commercial expert on the diplomatic staff of his country's embassy or large consulate in a foreign country.

commercial invoice A trade invoice.

commission agent *See* PURCHASING AGENT AND FOREIGN SALES REPRESENTATIVE.

Commodity Credit Corporation A government corporation controlled by the Department of Agriculture to provide financing and stability to the marketing and exporting of agricultural commodities.

commodity groupings A numerical system used by the United States Bureau of the Census to group imports and exports in broader categories than are provided by the tariff schedules. Currently, Schedule A is used to categorize imports, Schedule E for exports. Schedule B was replaced by Schedule E in 1978. *Compare* THE CUS-

TOMS COOPERATIVE COUNCIL NOMENCLATURE, STANDARD IN-
DUSTRIAL CLASSIFICATION, TARIFF SCHEDULES.

common carrier An individual, partnership, or corporation
which transports persons or goods for compensation.

compensation A form of countertrade in which the seller
agrees to take full or partial payment in goods or services
generated from the sale.

commission representative *See* FOREIGN SALES REPRE-
SENTATIVE.

conference line A member of a steamship conference. *See*
STEAMSHIP CONFERENCE.

confirmed letter of credit Issued by a bank abroad whose
validity and terms are confirmed to the beneficiary in the
United States by a United States bank.

consignee The person, firm, or representative to whom a
seller or shipper sends merchandise and who, upon presentation of the necessary documents, is recognized as the
owner of the merchandise for the purpose of the payment
of customs duties. This term is also used as applying to one
to whom goods are shipped, usually at the shipper's risk,
when an outright sale has not been made. *See* CONSIGN-
MENT.

consignee marks *See* MARKS.

consignment A term pertaining to merchandise shipped to a
consignee abroad when an actual purchase has not been
made, under an agreement by which the consignee is
obligated to sell the goods for the account of the consignor,
and to remit proceeds as goods are sold.

consul A government official residing in a foreign country who
is charged with the representation of the interests of his
country and its nationals.

consular declaration A formal statement, made to the consul of a foreign country, describing goods to be shipped.

consuler invoice A detailed statement regarding the character of goods shipped, duly certified by the consul of the
importing country at the port of shipment.

consulate The official premises of a foreign government representative.

contingency insurance Insurance taken out by the exporter
complementary to insurance bought by the consignee
abroad.

correspondent bank A bank which is a depositor in another bank, accepting and collecting items for its bank.

counterpurchase One of the most common forms of countertrade in which the seller receives cash but contractually agrees to buy local products or services as a percentage of cash received and over an agreed period of time.

countertrade International trade in which the seller is required to accept goods or other instruments of trade, in partial or whole payment for its products.

countervailing duty An extra duty imposed by the Secretary of Commerce to offset export grants, bounties, or subsidies paid to foreign suppliers in certain countries by the government of those countries as an incentive to export.

country of origin The country in which a particular commodity is manufactured.

credit risk insurance A form of insurance which covers the seller against loss due to nonpayment on the part of the buyer.

customs The duties levied by a country on imports and exports. The term also applies to the procedures and organization involved in such collection.

customhouse broker An individual or firm licensed to enter and clear through customs.

d/a *See* DOCUMENTS AGAINST ACCEPTANCE.

d/p *See* DOCUMENTS AGAINST PAYMENT.

date draft A draft drawn to mature on a specified number of days after the date it is issued, with or without regard to the date of acceptance.

delivery point *See* SPECIFIC DELIVERY POINT.

demurrage Excess time taken for loading or unloading a vessel as a result of a shipper. Charges are assessed by the shipping company.

Department of Commerce An agency of government whose purpose it is to promote commercial industrial interests in the country. *See* UNITED STATES DEPARTMENT OF COMMERCE.

destination control statement Any one of various statements which the United States Government requires to be displayed on export shipments and which specify the destination for which export of the shipment has been authorized.

devaluation The official lowering of the value of one country's currency in terms of one or more foreign currencies. Thus, if the United States dollar is devaluated in relation to the French Franc, one dollar will buy fewer francs than before.

developed countries   A term used to distinguish the more industrialized nations—including all OECD member countries as well as the Soviet Union and most of the socialist countries of Eastern Europe—from developing— or less developed—countries. The developed countries are sometimes collectively designated as the "North," because most of them are in the Northern Hemisphere.

developing countries (lcds)   A broad range of countries that generally lack a high degree of industrialization, infrastructure and other capital investment, sophisticated technology, widespread literacy, and advanced living standards among their populations as a whole. The developing countries are sometimes collectively designated as the "South," because a large number of them are in the Southern Hemisphere. All of the countries of Africa (except South Africa), Asia and Oceania (except Australia, Japan and New Zealand), Latin America, and the Middle East are generally considered "developing countries," as are a few European countries (Cyprus, Malta, Turkey, and Yugoslavia, for example). Some experts differentiate four subcategories of developing countries as having different economic needs and interest:

1) A few relatively wealthy OPEC countries—sometimes referred to as oil exporting developing countries—share a particular interest in a financially sound international economy and open capital markets;

2) Newly Industrializing Countries (NIC's) have a growing stake in an open international trading system;

3) A number of middle income countries—principally commodity exporters—have shown a particular interest in commodity stabilization schemes; and

4) More than 30 very poor countries ("least developed countries") are predominantly agricultural, have sharply limited development prospects during the near future, and tend to be heavily dependent on official development assistance. *See* LEAST DEVELOPED NATIONS.

disc   *See* DOMESTIC INTERNATIONAL CORPORATION.

discount (financial)   A deduction from the face value of commercial paper in consideration of cash by the seller before a specified date.

discrepancy—letter of credit When documents presented do not conform to the terms of the Letter of Credit, it is referred to as a discrepancy.

dispatch An amount paid by a vessel's operator to a charterer if loading or unloading is completed in less time than stipulated in the charter party.

distributor A firm that sells directly for a manufacturer, usually on an exclusive contract for a specified territory, and who maintains an inventory on hand.

dock receipt A receipt issued by an ocean carrier or its agent, acknowledging that the shipment has been delivered, or received at the dock or warehouse of the carrier.

documentary credit *see* LETTER OF CREDIT (COMMERCIAL).

documentary draft A draft to which documents are attached.

documentation/documents *See* SHIPPING DOCUMENTS.

documents against acceptance (d/a) A type of payment for goods in which the documents transferring title to the goods are not given to the buyer until he has accepted the draft issued against him.

documents against payment (d/p) A type of payment for goods in which the documents transferring title to the goods are not given to the buyer until he has paid the value of a draft issued against him.

Domestic International Sales Corporation (DISC) An export sales corporation set up by a United States company under United States Government authorization to promote exports from the United States by giving the exporter economic advantages not available outside such authorization.

domicile The place where draft or acceptance is made payable.

draft The same as a bill of exchange. A written order for a certain sum of money to be transferred on a certain date from the person who owes the money or agrees to make the payment (the drawee) to the creditor to whom the money is owed (the drawer of the draft). *See* DATE DRAFT, DOCUMENTARY DRAFT, SIGHT DRAFT, TIME DRAFT.

drawback (Import) The repayment, up to 99%, of customs duties paid on merchandise which later is exported, as part of a finished product, is known as a drawback. It refers also to a refund of a domestic tax which has been paid upon exportation of imported merchandise.

drawee One on whom a draft is drawn, and who owes the stated amount. *See* DRAFT.

drawer One who draws a draft, and receives payment. *See* DRAFT.

dumping Exporting merchandise into a country (e.g., the United States) at prices below the prices in the domestic market.

duty The tax imposed by a government on merchandise imported from another country.

Edge Act Corporation Banks that are subsidiaries to bank holding companies or other banks established to engage in foreign business transactions. They were established by an Act of Congress in 1919.

eurodollars United States dollars placed on deposit in banks outside the United States (primarily in Europe).

ex "from" (Point of Origin) A pricing term ("Ex Factory," "Ex Warehouse," etc) under which the seller agrees to place the goods at the buyer's disposal at the agreed place, with costs from that point being paid by the buyer.

exchange permit A governmental permit sometimes required of an importer to enable him to convert his own country's currency into foreign currency with which to pay a seller in another country.

exchange regulations/restrictions Restrictions imposed by an importing country to protect its foreign exchange reserves. *See* EXCHANGE PERMIT.

exchange rate The price of one currency in terms of another, i.e., the number of units of one currency that may be exchanged for one unit of another currency.

Eximbank The Export/Import Bank of the United States in Washington, DC.

excise tax A domestic tax assessed on the manufacture, sale, or use of a commodity within a country. Usually refundable if the product is exported.

expiration date The final date upon which the presentation of documents and drawing of drafts under a letter of credit may be made.

export To send goods to a foreign country or overseas territory.

export broker One who brings together the exporter and

importer for a fee and then withdraws from the transaction.

export declaration *See* SHIPPER'S EXPORT DECLARATION.

export license A governmental permit required to export certain products to certain destinations.

Export Management Company (EMC) A firm which acts as local export sales agent for several noncompeting manufacturers. (Term synonymous with "Manufacturer's Export Agent").

export merchant A producer or merchant who sells directly to a foreign purchaser without going through an intermediate such as an export broker.

Export Trading Company Act The law passed this act on October 8, 1982, designing it to encourage the formation of Export Trading Companies. It establishes an Office of Export Trading Company Affairs in Commerce, permits bankers' banks and holding companies to invest in ETCs, reduces the restrictions on export financing provided by financial institutions, and modifies the application of the antitrust laws to certain export trade.

export trading company An ETC, as envisioned by the ETC Act, is a company doing business in the United States principally to export goods or services produced in the United States or to facilitate such exports by unaffiliated persons. It can be owned by foreigners and can import, barter, and arrange sales between third countries, as well as export.

factoring A method used by businesses, including trading companies, to obtain cash for discounted accounts receivables or other assets.

f.a.s. free along side, as in fas (vessel) A pricing term under which the seller must deliver the goods to a pier and place them within reach of the ship's loading equipment.

FCIA Foreign Credit Insurance Association.

f.i.—"free in" A pricing term indicating that the charterer of a vessel is responsible for the cost of loading goods into the vessel.

f.o.—"free out" A pricing term indicating that the charterer of a vessel is responsible for the cost of loading goods from the vessel.

floating policy *See* OPEN POLICY.

f.o.b. free on board, as in f.o.b. (vessel) A pricing term under which the seller must deliver the goods on board the ship at the point named at his own expense. Similar terms are "F.O.B. (Destination)" and "F.O.B. (Named Point of Exportation)."

force majeure The title of a standard clause in marine contracts exempting the parties for nonfulfillment of their obligations as a result of conditions beyond their control, such as earthquakes, floods or war.

Foreign Credit Insurance Association (FCIA) An association of fifty insurance companies which operate in conjunction with the EXIMBANK to provide comprehensive insurance for exporters against nonpayment. FCIA underwrites the commercial credit risks. EXIMBANK covers the political risk and any excessive commercial risks.

foreign distribution *See* DISTRIBUTOR.

foreign exchange A currency or credit instruments of a foreign country. Also, transactions involving purchase and/or sale of currencies.

foreign freight forwarder *See* FREIGHT FORWARDER.

foreign sales agent An individual or firm that serves as the foreign representative of a domestic supplier and seeks sales abroad for the supplier.

foreign sales representative A representative or agent residing in a foreign country who acts as a salesman for a United States manufacturer, usually for a commission. Sometimes referred to as a "sales agent" or "commission agent." *See* REPRESENTATIVE.

foreign trade zone An area where goods of foreign origin may be brought in for reexport or transhipment without the payment of customs duty.

foul bill of lading A receipt for goods issued by a carrier bearing a notation that the outward containers or goods have been damaged. *See* CLEAN BILL OF LADING.

f.p.a.—"free of particular average" The title of a clause used in marine insurance, indicating that partial loss or damage to a foreign shipment is not covered. (Note: Loss resulting from certain conditions, such as the sinking or burning of the ship, may be specifically exempted from the effect of the clause.) Compare with W.P.A.

FSC—"foreign sales corporation" The Foreign Sales Corporation (FSC) replaces the DISC. To qualify for special tax treatment, an FSC must be a foreign corporation, maintain a summary of its permanent books of accounting at the foreign office, and have at least one director resident outside of the United States. A portion of the foreign sales corporation's income (generally corresponding to the tax deferred income of the DISC) would be exempt from United States tax at both the FSC and the United States corporate parent levels. This exemption is achieved by allowing a domestic corporation that is an FSC shareholder a 100% deduction for a portion of dividends received from an FSC attributable to economic activity actually conducted outside the United States customs territory. Interest, dividends, royalties, or other investment income of an FSC would be subject to United States tax.

free port An area generally encompassing a port and its surrounding locality into which goods may enter duty-free or subject only to minimal revenue tariffs.

free sale *See* CERTIFICATE OF FREE SALE.

free trade zone *See* FOREIGN TRADE ZONE.

freight forwarder An agent who assists his exporter client in moving cargo to a foreign destination.

General Agreement on Tariffs and Trade (GATT) The General Agreements on Tariffs and Trade is a multilateral trade treaty among governments, embodying rights and obligations. The detailed rules set out in the agreement constitute a code which the parties to the agreement have agreed upon to govern their trading relationships.

general license (export) Government authorization to export without specific documentary approval.

gross weight Total weight of goods, packing, and container, ready for shipment.

handling charges The forwarder's fee to his shipper client.

import To bring merchandise into a country from another country or overseas territory.

import license A governmental document which permits the importation of a product or material into a country where such licenses are necessary.

in bond A term applied to the status of merchandise admitted provisionally into a country without payment of duties. *See* BONDED WAREHOUSE.

inconvertibility The inability to exchange the currency of one country for the currency of another.

inherent vice Defects or characteristics of a product that could lead to deterioration without outside influence. An insurance term. *See* ALL RISK CLAUSE.

inland bill of lading A bill of lading used in transporting goods overland to the exporter's international carrier. Although a through bill of lading sometimes can be used, it is usually necessary to prepare both an inland bill of lading and an ocean bill of lading for export shipments. *Compare* AIR WAYBILL, OCEAN BILL OF LADING, THROUGH BILL OF LADING.

international freight forwarder *See* FREIGHT FORWARDER.

International Trade Administration (ITA) The ITA is a division of the Department of Commerce designed to promote world trade and to strengthen the international trade and investment position of the United States.

inland carrier A transportation line which handles export or import cargo between the port and inland points.

insurance certificate A document issued by an insurance company, usually to order of shipper under a marine policy, and insuring a particular shipment of merchandise.

invoice *See* COMMERCIAL INVOICE.

irrevocable Applied to letters of credit. An irrevocable letter of credit is one which cannot be altered or cancelled once it has been negotiated between the buyer and his bank.

joint venture A commercial or industrial arrangement in which principals of one company share control and ownership with principals of another.

least developed countries (ldcs) Some 36 of the world's poorest countries, considered by the United Nations to be the least developed of the less developed countries. Most of them are small in terms of area and population, and some are land-locked or small island countries. They generally are characterized by low per capita incomes, literacy levels, and medical standards, subsistence agriculture, and a lack of exploitable minerals and competitive industries. Many suffer from aridity, floods, hurricanes, and excessive animal and plant pests, and most are situated in the zone 10 to 30 degrees north latitude. These countries have little prospect of rapid economic development in the foreseeable future and are likely to remain heavily dependent upon official development assistance for many years. Most are in Africa, but a few, such as Bangladesh, Afghanistan, Laos, and Nepal, are in Asia.

Haiti is the only country in the Western Hemisphere classified by the United Nations as "least developed."

legal weight The weight of the goods plus immediate wrappings which go along with the goods, e.g. contents of a tin can together with its can. *See* NET WEIGHT.

letter of credit (commercial) Abbreviated "L/C" A document issued by a bank at buyer's request in favor of a seller, promising an agreed amount of money on receipt by the bank of certain documents within a specified time.

license *See* EXCHANGE LICENSE. EXPORT LICENSE, IMPORT LICENSE, VALIDATED LICENSE.

licensing The grant or technical assistance service and or the use of product rights, such as a trademark in return for royalty payments.

lighter An open or covered barge towed by a tugboat and used mainly in harbors and inland waterways.

lighterage The loading or unloading of a ship by means of a barge, or lighter which because of shallow water permits the ship from coming to shore.

mea manufacturer's export agent *See* EXPORT MANAGEMENT COMPANY.

marine insurance An insurance which will compensate the owner of goods transported on the seas in the event of loss which cannot be legally recovered from the carrier. Also covers air shipments.

marks A set of letters, numbers, and/or geometric symbols, generally followed by the name of the port of destination, placed on packages for export for identification purposes.

maturity date The date upon which a draft or acceptance becomes due for payment.

most-favored-nation status All countries having this designation receive equal treatment with respect to customs and tariffs.

named point *See* SPECIFIC DELIVERY POINT.

net weight Weight of the goods alone without any immediate wrapping, e.g. the weight of the contents of a tin can without the weight of the can. *See* LEGAL WEIGHT.

nomenclature of the Customs Cooperation Council This term was known as the Brussels Classification Nomenclature prior to January 1, 1975. It is the customs tariff adhered to by most European countries and many other countries throughout the world, and only recently by the United States.

ocean bill of lading A bill of lading (B/L) indicating that the exporter consigns a shipment to an international carrier for transportation to a specified foreign market. Unlike an inland B/L, the ocean B/L also serves as a collection document. If it is a straight B/L, the foreign buyer can obtain the shipment from the carrier by simply showing proof of identity. If a negotiable B/L is used, the buyer must first pay for the goods, post a bond, or meet other conditions agreeable to the seller. *Compare* AIR WAYBILL, INLAND BILL OF LADING, THROUGH BILL OF LADING.

offset A variation of countertrade in which the seller is required to assist in or arrange for the marketing of locally-produced goods.

on board bill of lading A bill of lading in which a carrier acknowledges that goods have been placed on board a certain vessel.

open account A trade arrangement in which goods are shipped to a foreign buyer without guarantee of payment. The obvious risk this method poses to the supplier makes it essential that the buyer's integrity be unquestionable.

open insurance policy A marine insurance policy that applies to all shipments made by an exporter over a period of time rather than to one shipment only.

open cargo policy *Synonymous with* FLOATING POLICY. An insurance policy which binds the insurer automatically to protect with insurance all shipments made by the insured from the moment the shipment leaves the initial shipping point until delivered at destination. The insuring conditions include clauses naming such risks insured against as "Perils of the sea"—fire, jettison, forcible theft, and barratry. *See* PERILS OF THE SEA, BARRATRY, ALL RISKS CLAUSE.

OPIC (Overseas Private Investment Corporation) A wholly-owned government corporation designed to promote private United States investment in developing countries by promoting political risk insurance and some financing assistance.

"order" bill of lading A negotiable bill of lading made out to the order of the shipper.

packing list A list which shows number and kinds of packages being shipped, totals of gross, legal and net weights of the packages, and marks and numbers on the packages. The list might be requested by an importer or might be required by an importing country to facilitate the clearance of goods through customs.

parcel post receipt The postal authorities' signed acknowledgement of delivery to them of a shipment made by parcel post.

perils of the sea A marine insurance term used to designate heavy weather, straining, lightning, collision, and sea water damage.

phytosanitary inspection certificate A certificate, issued by the United States Department of Agriculture, to satisfy import regulations of foreign countries, indicating that a United States shipment has been inspected and is free from harmful pests and plant diseases.

piggybacking The assigning of export marketing and distribution functions by one manufacturer to another.

port marks *See* MARKS.

pro forma invoice An invoice forwarded by the seller of goods prior to shipment to advise the buyer of the weight and value of the goods.

purchasing agent An agent who purchases goods in his/her own country on behalf of large foreign buyers such as government agencies and large private concerns.

procuring agent *See* PURCHASING AGENT.

quota The total quantity of a product or commodity which may be imported into a country without restriction or the penalty of additional duties or taxes.

quotation An offer to sell goods at a stated price and under stated terms.

rate of exchange The basis upon which money of one country will be exchanged for that of another. Rates of exchange are established and quoted for foreign currencies on the basis of the demand, supply, and stability of the individual currencies. *See* EXCHANGE.

representative The word "representative" is preferred to the word "agent" in writing, since "agent", in an exact legal sense, connotes more binding powers and responsibilities than "representative". *See* FOREIGN SALES REPRESENTATIVE.

revocable Applies to letters of credit. A revocable letter of credit is one which can be altered or cancelled by the buyer after he has opened it through his bank. *See* IRREVOCABLE.

royalty payment   The share of the product or profit paid by a licensee to his licensor. *See* LICENSING.

s.a. (*societe anonyme*)   French expression meaning a corporation.

sales agent   *See* FOREIGN SALES REPRESENTATIVE.

sales representative   *See* FOREIGN SALES REPRESENTATIVE.

sanitary certificate   A certificate which attests to the purity or absence of disease or pests in the shipment of food products, plants, seeds, and live animals.

Schedule B   Refers to "Schedule B, Statistical Classification of Domestic and Foreign Commodities Exported from the United States."

s/d   *See* SIGHT DRAFT.

Sherman Act   This law bars contracts, combinations, or conspiracies in restraint of trade and makes it a violation of law to monopolize or attempt to, or conspire to monopolize any trade in interstate or foreign commerce. Jurisdiction requires a direct, substantial, and reasonably foreseeable effect on domestic trade or commerce or on the export commerce of a person engaged in such commerce in the United States.

Shippers Export Declaration   A form required by the United States Treasury Department and completed by a shipper showing the value, weight, consignee, destination, etc. of export shipments as well as Schedule B identification number.

shippers documents   Commercial invoices, bills of lading, insurance certificates, consular invoices, and related documents.

ship's manifest   A true list in writing of the individual shipments comprising the cargo of a vessel, signed by the captain.

SIC   *See* STANDARD INDUSTRIAL CLASSIFICATION.

sight draft (s/d)   A draft so drawn as to be payable upon presentation to the drawee or at a fixed or determinable date thereafter. *See* DOCUMENTS AGAINST ACCEPTANCE, DOCUMENTS AGAINST PAYMENT.

SITC   *See* STANDARD INTERNATIONAL TRADE CLASSIFICATION.

specific delivery point   A point in sales quotations which designates specifically where and within what geographical locale the goods will be delivered at the expense and responsibility of the seller; e.g., F.A.S. named vessel at named port of export.

spot exchange The purpose or sale of foreign exchange for immediate delivery.

Standard Industrial Classification (SIC) A numerical system developed by the United States Government for the classification of commercial services and industrial products. Also classifies establishments by type of activity.

Standard International Trade Classification (SITC) A numerical system developed by the United Nations to classify commodities used in international trade as an and to reporting trade statistics.

state-controlled trading company In a country with a state trading monopoly, a trading entity empowered by the country's government to conduct export business.

steamship conference A group of vessel operators joined together for the purpose of establishing freight rates. A shipper might receive reduced rates if the shipper enters into a contract to ship on vessels of conference members only.

stocking distributor A distributor who maintains an inventory of goods of a manufacturer.

straight bill of lading A bill of lading, nonnegotiable, in which the goods are consigned directly to a named consignee.

swap arrangements A form of countertrade in which the seller sells on credit and then transfers the credit to a third party.

switch arrangements A form of countertrade in which the seller sells on credit and then transfers the credit to a third party.

tare weight The weight of packing and containers without the goods to be shipped.

tariff A schedule or system of duties imposed by a government on goods imported or exported, the rate of duty imposed in a tariff.

tariff schedules of the united states (tsus) A standard numerical system used by the United States Customs Bureau to classify imports and exports. *Compare* STANDARD INDUSTRIAL CLASSIFICATION,   CUSTOMS COOPERATION COUNCIL NOMENCLATURE, STANDARD INDUSTRIAL TRADE CLASSIFICATION.

TDP   *See* TRADE AND DEVELOPMENT PROGRAM.

tenor   The time fixed or allowed for payment, as in "the tenor of a draft."

through bill of lading   A single bill of lading covering the domestic and international carriage of an export shipment. An air waybill, for instance, is essentially a through bill of lading used for air shipments. Ocean shipments, on the other hand, usually require two separate documents— an inland bill of lading for domestic carriage and an ocean bill of lading for international carriage. Through bills of lading, therefore, cannot be used. *Compare* AIR WAYBILL, INLAND BILL OF LADING, OCEAN BILL OF LADING.

time draft   A draft drawn so it matures at a certain fixed time after presentation or acceptance.

United States standard master   A single business form with correctable stencil which includes space for information required on many different export forms. Use of this form enables multiple typing.

Trade Development Program (TDP)   This program is designed to promote economic development in the Third World and the sale of United States goods and services to these developing countries. It operates as part of the International Development Cooperative Agency.

trade mission   A mission to a foreign country organized to promote trade through the establishment of contracts and exposure to the commercial environment. They are frequently organized by federal, state, or local agencies.

tramp steamer   A ship not operating on regular routes or schedules.

trust receipt   Release of merchandise by a bank to a buyer in which the bank retains title to the merchandise. The buyer, who obtains the goods for manufacturing or sales purposes, is obligated to maintain the goods (or the proceeds from their sale) distinct from the remainder of his/her assets and to hold them ready for repossession by the bank.

turnkey   A method of construction whereby the contractor assumes total responsibility from design through completion of the task.

validated license   A government document authorizing the export of commodities within limitations set forth in the document.

vertical etc An ETC that integrates a range of functions taking products from suppliers to consumers.

visa A signature of formal approval on an entree document. Obtained from a consulate.

w.a.—"with average" A marine insurance term meaning that a shipment is protected from partial damage whenever the damage exceeds 3% (or some other percentage).

warehouse receipt A receipt issued by a warehouse listing goods received for storage.

Webb-Pomerene Association Institutions engaged in exporting that combine the products of similar producers for overseas sales. These associations have partial exemption from United States antitrust laws but may not engage in third country trade or combine to export services. *See* HORIZONTAL ETCS.

wharfage Charge assessed by carrier for the handling of incoming or outgoing ocean cargo.

without reserve A term indicating that a shipper's agent or representative is empowered to make definitive decisions and adjustments abroad without approval of the group individual represented. *Compare* ADVISORY CAPACITY.

Index

Index

A

absolute quotas, 135
accounting, 140
advertising, 31
Agency for International Development (AID), 55
agency/distributor agreements, 69
agent/distributor service (ADS), 100
agricultural commodities, importing to U.S., 136
air transportation, 70
air waybill, 90
antidumping laws, 113
armaments, importing to U.S., 136
Asia, 3
authority to purchase, 58

B

bad credit avoidance, 65-66
Bain, Alexander, 44
balance sheet, 146, 148, 150
bank drafts, 58
bank financing, 52, 156
banker's acceptances, 52
bargaining, 34
beginning transactions, 6-26
big ticket items, 22
bill of exchange, 35
bill of lading, 58, 76, 86, 92, 93
blanket protection, 68
bonds, 119
bottom line, pricing for, 20
breakage, 72
bribes, 36
Brussels Tariff Nomenclature (BTN), 126
budgets, 155
Business America, 98
business cycles, 157
business name, 139
business plan, 143-148, 154
business risk avoidance, 56

C

C.I.F., 18
cablegrams, 41, 43
Canada, 2
capital, start-up, 139
carnets, 50, 103
cash flow, 146, 148, 151
cash in advance, 64
catalog shows, 31
certificate of manufacture, 79, 82
certificate of marine insurance, 84
certificate of origin, 75, 76, 77
Chambers of Commerce, U.S., 12, 18
China, 3
classification of goods, importing to U.S., 125
clean on board bill of lading, 93
collection documents, 76
Commerce, Department of, 12, 115, 116, 157
Commercial Information Management Systems (CIMS), 97
commercial invoice, 58, 76, 78
Commercial News USA, 99
commercial attache, 77
commercial invoice, 77
commissions, 21
commitment, 153
commodity control list (CCL), 106
communications, 38-46, 156
comparison shopping service, 99
competition, 155
completion of transactions, 51-93
confirmation, 60
consignment, 57
consular invoice, 76, 77, 80
consumer products, importing to U.S., 136
contacting overseas markets, 10
Contacts Influential, 118
contracts, 34
conventions, 103, 117

187

copyrights, 137
cosmetics, importing to U.S., 136
cost, insurance, freight (C.I.F.), 18
costing worksheets, import and export, 24-25
counterpurchase, 35
countertrade, 35
covering, 68
credit, bad, avoidance of, 65-66
cultural obstacles, 153
currency, importing to U.S., 136
customhouse broker, 118-119, 156
   license application for, 120
Customs Attache, 116
Customs Cooperation Council (CCC), 126
customs invoice, 58
Customs Service, 115, 116, 119, 161
   U.S. Districts of, 162

D
decision-making units, 29, 157
delivery points, 18
developed countries (DCs), 9
direct distance dial (DDD), 39
direct sales, 30
Directory of Manufacturers' Agents, 117
Directory of the United States Importers, 117
distributors, 32, 117, 157
District Export Councils (DEC), 96
documentation, 74-93
Domestic International Sales Corporations (DISC), 111
drafts, 35
drugs, importing to U.S., 136

E
employees, 141
Encyclopedia of Associations, 117
European Community, 3, 100
EX, 20
examination of goods, importing to U.S., 121
exhibits, 117
EXIMBANK, 54, 67, 103
expenses, 141
export licenses, 82
export management companies (EMC), 102
export trading company, 112
Export-Import bank, 54, 67, 103
exporting from U.S., 1, 94, 114
   books on, 102
   controls for, 105
   costing worksheet, 24
   European community, impact of, 100
export license application form, 107-110
freight forwarders, 103-105
government information sources, 97
government support, 95
guide to, 102
information sources, 96
market research checklist, 12-14
shipper, 104
tax incentives for, 111-114
unfair practices, protection from, 113
exposure, 68

F
F.A.S., 18
F.O.B., 18
facilitating payments, 36
facsimile (FAX), 44
factors, 53
federal maritime commission (FMC), 104
financial data, 146
financial records, 140
financing, 51-55
follow-up communications, 39
food, importing to U.S., 136
food and drink, overseas, 48
Foreign Traders Index (FTI), 99
foreign business organizations, 158
Foreign Commercial Service (FCS), 95, 116
Foreign Corrupt Practices Act (FCPA), 35
Foreign Credit Insurance Association (FCIA), 67
foreign exchange, risk avoidance, 68
foreign sales corporations (FSC), 111
foreign trade data, 101
forward exchange rate, 68
foul bill, 93
free alongside ship (F.A.S.), 18
free on board (F.O.B), 18
freight forwarder, 103-105, 156
FT 410 data, 101
future exchange rate, 68

G
General Agreement on Tariff and Trade (GATT), 2, 3, 111
general license, 105
global market surveys (GMS), 99
gold, importing to U.S., 136
Guide to Documentary Operations, A, 59

H
Harmonized Commodity Description and Coding System, 126

Harmonized System (HS) Tariff Schedule, 125
hedging, 68
hotels, 48

I

import quotas, 135
Importing into the United States, 116
importing to U.S., 1, 115-137
  agricultural commodities, 136
  arms, munitions, radioactive material, 136
  classification of goods, 125
  consumer products, 136
  costing worksheet, 25
  customhouse brokers, 118-119
  entry process, 121
  examination of goods, 121
  foods, drugs, cosmetics, medical devices, 136
  gold, silver, currency, stamps, 136
  government support, 115
  Harmonized System (HS) Tariff Schedule, 125
  Harmonized System (HS) Tariff Schedule, case study, 127, 128, 132, 135
  import quotas, 135
  information sources for, 116-118
  liquidation, 125
  market research checklist, 14-15
  pesticides, toxic and hazardous substances, 137
  special regulations, 135
  tariffs, 119
  textiles, wool, fur, 137
  trademarks, tradenames, copyrights, 137
  valuation of goods, 122
  wildlife and pets, 137
income statement, 149
INCOTERMS, 18
independent shipping lines, 70
indirect sales, 30
industrial sector analysis, 99
industry-oriented, government approved trade missions, 31
information sources, 154, 163
initial quotes, 15-20
inspection certificate, 76, 83, 86
insurance, 67-68, 142
  marine, 18, 70, 84
insurance certificate, 83
intellectual property rights, 36
intermodalism, 71
Internal Revenue Service (IRS), 140
International Development Cooperation Agency (IDCA), 55
international market research surveys (IMR), 99

international record carriers (IRCs), 41
international trade, 1-3
  entering into, 4-5
  global changes in, 3-4
  market nations for, 5
  opportunities in, 5
International Trade Administration (ITA), 95
  district offices, U.S., 160
  embassy missions of, 159
International Trade Commission (ITC), 113
introductory letters, 38, 40
invoices, 58, 76, 77
irrevocable credit, 60

J

jet lag, 48
Journal of Commerce, 98

L

labeling, 72
land bridge, 71
land transportation, 71
launching profitable transaction, 6-26
least developed countries (LDCs), 9
letters of credit, 59-64
licenses, 82, 105, 140
liquidation, importing to U.S., 125
load centering, 71

M

macrosegmentation, 29
mailgrams, 41
Major Mass-Market Merchandise, 118
management, 155
Manufacturers' Agents Annual Directory, 118
marginal-cost pricing, 21
marine insurance, 18, 70, 84
market channels, 20
Market Guide of Mass Merchandisers, 117
market research, 7, 12-15, 154
marketing and market plan, 8-10, 28-33, 146, 155, 157
  checklist for, 32-33
  contacts for, 10, 11
  execution of, 29
  overseas, 72
markets, segmenting, 28
marking, 72, 73
medical devices, importing to U.S., 136
Mexico, 2
micro-bridge, 71
microsegmentation, 29
middlemen, 30

minibridge, 71
Modern Packaging Encyclopedia, 72
moisture and weather damage, 72
munitions, importing to U.S., 136

N
National Council of American Importers, 18
National Foreign Trade council, 18
negotiations, 27, 34-38
network services, 41

O
ocean bill of lading, 92
ocean conference, 70
Official Airlines Guide (OAG), 47
office and office supplies, 141
Office of Business Liason (OBL), 97
Office of Export Development, 98
open account, 57
order bill of lading, 86
organization of business, 139
Overseas Private Investment Corporation (OPIC), 67, 102
overseas trade promotions calendar, 98

P
packaging, 72
packing, 69, 72
packing lists, 83, 87
partners, overseas and domestic, 157
patents, 36, 37
payments, 56
personal sales, 30
pesticides, importing to U.S., 137
pets, importing to U.S., 137
physical distribution, 69
pilferage, 72
planning, 27, 154
political risks, 67
precious metals, importing to U.S., 136
pricing, 20-21
Private Export Funding Corporation (PEFCO), 53
pro forma invoice, 15-17
products
  alternative uses for, 9
  life cycle of, 9
  researching appeal of, 8, 155
  standards of quality for, 8
professional exhibitions, 103
profit and loss, 146, 148

Q
qualified general license, 105
quality control, 9

quantitative quotas, 135
quotas, import, 135

R
radioactive material, importing to U.S., 136
request for quotation (RFQ), 15
research, 7, 154
resource analysis, 146
revocable credit, 60
risk avoidance, 55-74
RO/RO, 71

S
sales, 30
sales projection worksheet, pro forma, 147, 148
secured financing, 52
segmenting markets, 28
seller's permit, 140
seminar trade missions, 31
service bureaus, 45
Service Corps of Retired Executives (SCORE), 142
setting up import/export business, 138-152
  accounting, 140
  business organization, 139
  business plan, 143-148
  checklist for, 142
  employees, 141
  financial records and data, 140, 146
  insurance, 142
  licenses, 140
  marketing strategies, 146
  name, 139
  office and office supplies, 141
  resources, analysis of, 146
  review, rewrite, implement, 148
  seller's permit, 140
  short- and long-term goals, 146
  start-up capital, 139
  support teams, 142
shippers, 104
shippers export declaration, 83, 88, 106
shipping, 69, 70
  checklist for, 74
  documentation for, 74
  insurance for, 67
shipping documents, 35
sight draft, 58
silver, importing to U.S., 136
Small Business Administration (SBA), 54, 142
sourcing, contacts for, 10
Soviet Union, 3
Special Permit for Immediate Delivery, 121-123

special trade missions, 31
specific delivery point, 18
spot market, 68
stamps, importing to U.S., 136
start-up capital, 139
store-and-forward services, 41
straight bill of lading, 86
success tips, 153-157
support, 142
surety company, 119

T
Tariff Act of 1930, 116
Tariff Schedule of the United States
   (TSUS), 125-135
Tariff Schedule of the United States
   Annotated (TSUSA), 126, 131
tariff-rate quotas, 135
tariffs, 113, 119
   countries receiving free, 133-134
technical marketing decisions, 8-10
technical specifications and codes, 9
telephones, 39
telex, 38, 39, 41, 43
terminology, 7
terms of sale, 18
textiles, importing to U.S., 137
thefts, 72
*Thomas Register of American Manufac-
   turers*, 117
time (date) draft, 58
time changes, 48, 49
toxic and hazardous substances, importing to U.S., 137
Trade and Development Program (TDP),
   55
trade lists, 98
trade missions, 31
Trade Opportunities Program (TOP), 98

trade show or fairs, 11, 30, 98, 103, 117
Trade Shows and Convention Guide, 117
*Trade Shows and Professional Exhibits
   Directory*, 117
trademarks, 36, 38, 137
tradenames, 137
tramp vessels, 70
transaction values, 122
transmission times rates, 39
transportation, overseas, 47
travel, 47-50, 156
   arrival/departure tips, 50
   danger alerts, 47
   packing, 47
Treasury, Department of, 115

U
unfair import practices, 113
United States, 2
unsecured financing, 53
Uraguay Round, 3

V
validated license, 105
valuation of goods, importing to U.S., 122
video/catalog exhibitions, 31
visas, 48
volume, 26

W
water transportation, 70
waybills, 90
wildlife, importing to U.S., 137
wool and furs,importing to U.S., 137
world traders data reports (WTDRs), 99
Whalen, Richard, 1

About The Author

Dr. Carl A. Nelson is well qualified to write this book. He is a specialist in international trade and a professional writer.

He earned his Doctorate in Business Administration—Finance, (emphasis on international finance and trade), from the United States International University in San Diego, California. His Doctoral Dissertation—The Relationship of Export Obstacles to the Export Trading Company Act of 1982—focused on United States small business export problems. He is also a graduate of the Naval War College, holds a Master of Science degree in Management (Economics/Systems Analysis) from the Naval Post-graduate school in Monterey, California, and an engineering degree from the United States Naval Academy at Annapolis Maryland.

He is founder and principal of Global Business and Trade (GBT), an international business assistance and training company.

Dr. Nelson is also an Adjunct Professor of International Trade at United States International University (USIU) where he teaches undergraduate and graduate level courses. He gives seminars and workshops on the basics and applications of global trade.

His dominant international experience has been in Asia where he spent the major part of the past 25 years. He lived for two years in Japan, one year in South Vietnam, and is intimately knowledgeable about Hawaii, Guam, South Korea, Hong Kong, Australia, Philippines, New Zealand, and the Indian Ocean area. His most recent international work has been in Central America and along the California/Mexican border where he specializes in Maquiladora operations.

As a professional writer, he has published both fiction and nonfiction. His articles on international business matters have been published in Global Trade Executive, The Trader (monthly newsletter of the San Diego World Trade Association), and the Daily Transcript (the local San Diego business newspaper). He has written four books—three nonfiction and one war novel. In 1987 he won awards for both fiction and nonfiction.

Dr. Nelson is a former captain in the United States Navy. He commanded three war ships, one USN/VN combat riverine unit, a USN/VN logistic support base, and served four tours of duty in the Vietnamese war. He held demanding positions on major operational staffs as well as the staffs of the United States Military Academy at West Point and the United States Naval Academy at Annapolis, Maryland.